POCKET

KU-228-650

KINGFISHER

GUIDE TO THE

WILDLIFE

OF BRITAIN & EUROPE

JEANETTE HARRIS

KINGFISHER BOOKS

Advisers:
Michael Chinery
Naturalist, writer and broadcaster.

Esmond Harris .
Director of the Royal Forestry Society.

Richard Mabey
Writer, botanist and broadcaster.

Peter Olney
Curator of Birds, Zoological Society, London.

Derek Reid
Head of Mycology Department, Royal Botanic Gardens, Kew.

Kingfisher Books, Grisewood & Dempsey Ltd., Elsley House, 24–30 Great Titchfield Street, London W1P 7AD.

This edition published in 1988. Originally published in hardcover in 1981 as *Nature Handbook* by Kingfisher Books. Reprinted 1989
ⓒ Kingfisher Books Ltd 1981

BRITISH LIBRARY CATALOGUING IN PUBLICATION DATA
Harris, Jeanette
    Pocket guide to the wildlife of Britain & Europe. – 3rd ed. – (Kingfisher pocket books).
    1. Natural history – Great Britain
    I. Title II. Harris, Jeanette.
    Pocket guide to the wildlife of Britain & Europe.
    574.941   QH137
ISBN 0 86272 267 5

Printed and Bound in Italy by Vallardi Industrie Grafiche

Contents

INTRODUCTION 4

MAMMALS 6
Rabbit, Hares and Rodents 9
Rodents 10
Mole, Hedgehog and Shrews 12
Meat-eaters 13
Deer and other Hooved Animals 16
Bats 18
Seals, Porpoise and Dolphin 19

BIRDS 20
Shearwater, Fulmar, Gannet, Diver and Grebes 22
Cormorants, Heron, Bittern and Stork 23
Ducks 24
Geese and Swans 27
Birds of Prey 28
Game Birds 30
Crane, Rails and Crakes 32
Waders 33
Gulls 37
Gulls and Terns 38
Auks 39
Pigeon, Doves and Cuckoo 40
Owls 41
Nightjar, Swift, Kingfisher and Related Birds 42
Woodpeckers 43
Larks, Martins and Swallow 45
Crows and Oriole 46
Tits 48
Babbler, Nuthatch, Creeper, Wren and Dipper . 49
Thrushes, Chats and Redstarts 50
Warblers and Goldcrest 52
Flycatchers, Dunnock and Pipits 54
Wagtails, Waxwing, Shrikes and Starling 55
Finches 56
Buntings and Sparrows 58

AMPHIBIANS AND REPTILES 60
Lizards and Snakes 61
Frogs and Newts 62

FISHES 64
Freshwater Fishes 66
Coastal Fishes 70

INSECTS and other Invertebrates 72
Butterflies 74
Moths 79
Beetles 83
Bugs 85
Ants and Bees 86
Wasps 87
True Flies 88
Other Flies 89
Dragonflies 90
Other Insects 91
Other Invertebrates 92

SHELLS and other Seashore Creatures 94
Single Shells 96
Bivalves 98
Other Seashore Creatures 100

TREES 102
Larches 105
Cedars and Firs 106
Spruces 109
Pines 110
Redwoods 112
Cypresses 114
Other Evergreens 116
Poplars and Willows 118
Willow and Hazel 120
Alder and Birch 121
Hornbeam and Beech 122
Chestnut and Oak 123
Oaks 124
Maples and Plane 126
Horse Chestnut and Limes 128

Elms 129
Ash and Walnut 130
Rose Family 131
Pea Family 134
Elder, Holly and Olive 135

WILD FLOWERS 136
Buttercups 138
Poppies and Water-lilies 140
Fumitory and Cabbage Family 141
Violets, Milkwort and St John's Wort 142
Stitchworts 143
Goosefoot, Mallow and Wood Sorrel 145
Geraniums and Balsam 146
Pea Family 147
Rose Family 149
Rose Family and Stonecrop 150
Saxifrage, Grass of Parnassus, Loosestrife and Sundew 152
Willowherbs and Ivy 153
Carrot Family 154
Spurge and Docks 155
Nettle, Heather and Thrift 156
Primroses and Gentians 157
Borage Family 158
Bogbean, Bindweed and Nightshades 159
Figworts 160
Mints, Plantain and Bellflower 162
Bedstraws and Honeysuckle 164
Teasels and Valerian 165
Daisy Family 166
Lilies and Arum 171
Iris and Daffodils 172
Orchids 173

MUSHROOMS AND TOADSTOOLS 174
Fungi with Gills 175
Fungi with Tubes 182
Other Fungi 183

INDEX 184

Introduction

Learning about nature begins with looking – with noticing the differences between one tree, bird, flower, insect or fish and another. The *Pocket Guide* will help you to do this, and to identify those plants or animals you are most likely to see in Britain and northern Europe. In the book, which includes over 700 species, a wide variety of plants – trees, flowers and non-green plants or fungi – are illustrated and described, as well as many animals, including mammals, birds, fishes, seashore creatures, insects, amphibians and reptiles.

Each species is identified by its common as well as its scientific name. The common names can be confusing as there are often several for one plant or animal, and sometimes one name can apply to several different species. To avoid confusion, scientists have developed rules governing the use of scientific names. These are often called Latin names, but this is inaccurate, as some of the words are Greek. In scientific language, every species has a name made up of two parts. The first part is the 'generic' name e.g., *Pinus* (a pine

◀ The bumblebee is one of the many insects which pollinate flowering plants. The pollen sticks to the bee's fur and is later gathered by the bee into 'pollen baskets' on the hind legs.

▶ All plants and animals have adapted to make use of a particular habitat. Here alder thrives in wet conditions because it has special bacteria growing in root nodules which help it to live in waterlogged conditions.

tree) and is common to all pines. The second is the 'specific' name which refers to one species only e.g., *P. sylvestris*, Scots pine (which, despite its common name in English, is abundant throughout northern Europe and Scandinavia). The index includes' both common and scientific names.

Unless otherwise stated, the measurements given are the total length of the animal or the height of the plant. All measurements are the normal average of a mature plant or animal and are only a guide, as individuals can vary greatly. Colour and markings also vary. There are often colour differences between young and mature and, more often, between male and female of the same species. The symbols ♂ denoting male and ♀ denoting female are used throughout the book where there is a significant difference between the two.

Each area supports a particular network of wildlife, depending on its climate and geography. Different types of soil produce different plants, these plants are eaten by certain animals and these animals will be the food of other animals. In this way, a whole chain of life is set up, adapted to the environment or habitat — be it field, wood, marsh, river, mountain or coastline. Whichever part of the country you live in, you will gradually learn to know which plants and animals to expect there, and to trace the relationship between them.

Mammals

Mammals are a distinct group of animals that feed their young on milk secreted by special glands. The young are cared for by their mothers until they are old enough to look after themselves. Most mammals have hair, both soft under-fur to keep them warm and coarse outer hair, which helps to repel rain and keep the animal dry.

Mammals are divided into groups or orders according to their body structure and the way they live. The mammals in this book belong to the following orders:

The rodents (vole, mouse, rat, squirrel, coypu). These mammals have large front teeth called incisors, specially adapted for gnawing, which grow throughout their life. Most of these mammals are small and breed quickly, producing large numbers of young.

The insect-eaters (mole, hedgehog, shrew) have lots of small, pointed teeth for eating and crushing the insects and other small creatures on which they feed.

▼ **Badger** *Meles meles* 75–93cm. Immensely strong for its size, with a tenacious grip. Found nearly all over Europe.

The meat-eaters (fox, badger, otter, mink, stoat, weasel, polecat, marten, wild cat) have large, pointed 'eye' teeth or canines, used for stabbing and tearing up meat or fish, and powerful jaws.

The hooved mammals (deer, goat, sheep) have divided hooves and are animals which eat grass and other plants. They lack teeth at the front of the upper jaw, which is instead a hard pad the lower teeth bite against to tear up grass. The grass is swallowed, then later regurgitated for chewing into smaller fragments. Animals that eat in this way are called ruminants. Goats and sheep of both sexes have horns, but only male deer have antlers, which they shed once a year and regrow.

The flying mammals (bats) have wings supported by their limbs. Their food is caught in flight by echo location, their ears and noses being modified to emit and receive signals.

The seals have teeth like carnivores (meat-eaters), but their limbs have developed as flippers with which to swim. They can stay under water for long periods, rising regularly to the surface to breathe.

The dolphins and porpoises are adapted to living completely in water. Their limbs are streamlined, like fins, for swimming.

▼ **Chamois** *Rupicapra rupicapra*
110–130cm. Goat-like, with small, slender horns curved at the tips, and white markings. Lives in mountains in Europe.

CLUES AND HINTS

Food remains and droppings: Look out for cones attacked by squirrels, nuts gnawed by mice, fish bitten by otters. Deer and rabbit droppings are easily identified.

Animal homes: Look out for squirrel dreys in the forks of trees, rabbit holes and badger sets.

Sounds: Listen for the bark of a roe-deer, the high-pitched squeak of a shrew or bat.

Tracks: Look out for broad pads (badger) and oval ones (fox). Position varies if walking or running. (See page 8.)

Other signs: Shed antlers or frayed trees show that deer are about. Hairs caught in a fence can be identified with practice.

Measurements given are the total length of head, body and tail, though the length of tail is given separately where it is significant. Where appropriate the height to the shoulder is given. All measurements are averages and only a guide, as individuals vary greatly in size. Colour and markings also vary, and young animals are often very different from adults and are, of course, smaller.

Mammals are more difficult to observe than other animals as many are shy, small and only active at night or in the early morning. There is still a great deal to be found out about their habits and behaviour by the careful and patient amateur observer.

TRACKS

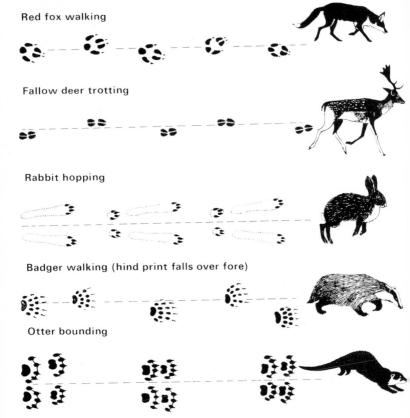

Red fox walking

Fallow deer trotting

Rabbit hopping

Badger walking (hind print falls over fore)

Otter bounding

Rabbit, Hares and Rodents

▶ **Rabbit** *Oryctolagus cuniculus* 35–45cm. Long ears, no black tips like hares. Long hind legs. White tail, easily seen when rabbit moves. Colour greyish-brown, white below, sometimes black. Hops, thumps back legs when alarmed. Lives in groups in burrows.

◀ **Brown Hare** *Lepus capensis* 48–67cm. Long ears with black tips. Light sandy-brown in colour, white underparts. Larger than rabbit with longer legs, so lopes rather than hops. When disturbed, runs very quickly, twisting and turning. Fields and open country.

▶ **Blue Hare** *Lepus timidus* 45–50cm. Black-tipped ears are shorter than brown hare, smaller and more rabbit-like. Grey in summer, turns white in winter except for ear tips. Mainly in upland areas.

▲ **Coypu** *Myocastor coypus* 42–60cm. Like large guinea pig with long thick tail. Often seen swimming when blunt nose, broad head and back show above the water. Webbed hind feet. Active dawn and dusk. Burrows in river banks.

▶ **Muskrat** *Ondatra zibethicus* 26–35cm. Tail flattened from side to side for swimming. Active night and early morning in still and slow-moving water with lots of weeds. Not in Britain.

9

Rodents

◀ **Grey Squirrel** *Sciurus carolinen*
Body 25–30cm, tail 20cm. Head
broader and more rat-like than red
squirrel. Summer coat is grey, with
red-brown on the flanks and white
underparts, winter coat grey, tail dark
grey. Some animals have more red-
brown in the coat than others. Ear tuft
not noticeable. Builds dreys in trees.
Mainly deciduous woods and
parklands.

▶ **Red Squirrel** *Sciurus vulgaris*
Body 20–22cm, tail 20cm. Smaller,
with narrower head than grey squirrel.
Tail bushier, becoming very light in
summer. Coat becomes greyer and ear
tufts longer during the winter. Darker
specimens in southern Europe. Prefers
woods with conifers, feeding on
shoots and cones.

◀ **Short-tailed Vole** *Microtus
agrestis* Body 9–12cm, tail 3–4cm.
Coat brown above, grey below. Rough
grassland, including moors and
marshes, and light woodland.
Sometimes in large numbers. Commo

◀ **Water Vole** *Arvicola terrestris*
Body 17–20cm, tail 9–12cm. Swims
with broad flat head and blunt nose
just above the water. Lives by and in
water.

▶ **Bank Vole** *Clethrionomys
glareolus* Body 9–12cm, tail 4–7cm.
Rich red-brown upper parts, creamy-
white underparts. Deciduous
woodland, hedgerows and gardens.

◀ **Wood Mouse** *Apodemus sylvaticus* Body 9cm, tail 8cm. Pointed muzzle, large eyes, ears and hind feet. Underparts grey or white, often with yellowish spot on chest. Nocturnal. Common.

◀ **Harvest Mouse** *Micromys minutus* Body 5–7cm, tail 6–7cm. Muzzle not pointed like other mice, head broader. Tail used for holding on to vegetation. Active mainly by day in tall, rough grassland and in cornfields.

◀ **House Mouse** *Mus musculus* Body 7–8cm, tail 7–8cm. Long pointed nose. Fur grey. Leaves a characteristic 'mousey' smell where present. Mainly nocturnal. Rarely far from man.

▶ **Dormouse** *Muscardinus avellanarius* Body 7cm, tail 6cm. Tail hairy unlike those of voles and mice. Hibernates October to April. Deciduous woodland, hedges.

▶ **Edible Dormouse** *Glis glis* Body 17cm, tail 15cm. Like young grey squirrel, but head mouse-like with bulging eyes. Nocturnal, lives in trees.

◀ **Brown Rat** *Rattus norvegicus* Body 22–28cm, tail 20cm. Tail thick and scaly. Large size distinguishes it from voles and mice. Characteristic smell. Often in large numbers. Occurs in fields and hedgerows in summer, many moving into buildings for the winter. Rarely far from human activity.

11

Mole, Hedgehog and Shrews

▲ **Mole** *Talpa europaea* Body 11–16cm, tail 3cm. Small eyes. Clawed, spade-like front feet. Dense velvety fur. Lives underground for most of the time.

▼ **Water Shrew** *Neomys fodiens* Body 7–9cm, tail 4–7cm. Fur is velvety, underparts usually white, upper parts blue-grey or dark brown. Near water.

▼ **Hedgehog** *Erinaceus-europaeus* 22–27cm. Easily distinguished by numerous black-tipped spines. Rarely seen before nightfall unless ill

▼ **White-toothed Shrew** *Crocidura russula* Body 6–9cm, tail 4cm. Teeth have no red tips like most other shrews. Woods, fields and gardens. Not in Britain.

◀ **Pygmy Shrew** *Sorex minutus* Body 5–6cm, tail 3–5cm. Tail long, at least two-thirds the body. Dark brown above, whitish below. Teeth have red tips.

▶ **Common Shrew** *Sorex araneus* Body 6–7cm, tail 3–5cm. Snout long, teeth red-tipped. Dark brown above, yellowish flanks, whitish beneath. Can often be heard squeaking.

Meat-eaters

▶ **Fox** *Vulpes vulpes* Body 60–80cm, tail 30–48cm. Leaves distinctive scent. Tracks dog-like, but pads oval. Male barks, female (vixen) screams. Digs a burrow (earth) or lives in badgers' sets. Largely nocturnal. Occurs throughout Britain and has become common in town suburbs.

◀ **Badger** *Meles meles* Body 67–80cm, tail 12–18cm. Not often seen in daylight except at sunset. Shuffles with body moving from side to side. Tracks show 5 oval pads with main central pad long and oval. A powerful animal, but eats mainly worms and plant food. Many badgers may live in one set – underground tunnels with several entrances. Copses and deciduous woods.

▶ **Otter** *Lutra lutra* Body 62–83cm, tail 35–55cm. Long body with powerful thick tail used for swimming. Broad flat head with small ears. Legs short with webbed feet. Webs can often be seen in the tracks together with the tail marks. Dense under fur prevents the body from getting wet. Eats fish. Mainly nocturnal. Usually near rivers or coasts.

13

Meat-eaters

▶ **Stoat** *Mustela erminea*
Body 22—29cm, tail 8—12cm.
Long bodied and sinuous,
with short legs. Foxy-red
above with distinct line
separating the white
underparts. In north, turns
white all over in winter except
for black tail tip (ermine).
Feeds on rabbits, voles, birds.
Kills by bite at back of neck.
In and around woods and
hedgerows.

Winter

▶ **Weasel** *Mustela nivalis* Body 17—
23cm, tail 4—7cm. Smaller than stoat
with shorter and less bushy tail which
has no black tip. Long body, sinuous,
with short legs. Head is narrower and
the line separating the upper parts from
the underparts is not as straight as in
the stoat. Often has brown spots on
underparts. Male larger than female.
Kills by bite at back of neck, feeding on
birds, mice, rats and voles. Found in
woodlands, farmland and open
country.

► **Pine Marten** *Martes martes*
Body 43–50cm, tail 20–26cm. A
cat-sized animal with a long body,
longer legs than a stoat and a long
bushy tail used in climbing trees,
like the squirrel. Ears large and
rounded, pointed snout. Colour is
rich brown with yellowish throat
patch. Male larger than female.
Found in woodland and also more
open areas. Beech marten *Martes
foina* similar but with white throat
patch.

◄ **Polecat** *Mustela
putorius* Body 30–
45cm, tail 12–18cm.
Like a large stoat with
dark brown or black fur
with a purplish shine.
Lighter on flanks, no
white underneath. Face
has whitish patches on
nose and behind eye.
Glands near tail produce
a pungent smell. Woods
and thickets.

◄ **Wild Cat** *Felis silvestris*
Body 48–75cm, tail 25–
35cm. The true wild cat is like
a large domestic tabby cat
with a pattern of bold tiger-
like stripes. Head broader,
tail thick, short and bushy
with black rings and black
tip. Hind-quarters more
powerful than domestic cat.
Wild cat will breed with
domestic cat so that a range
of types may be found.
British ones occur in
Scotland only.

15

Deer and other Hooved Animals

◄ **Roe Deer** *Capreolus capreolus* 65–75cm high at shoulder. Small goat-sized deer. Broad heart-shaped white or yellow rump. Coat is grey in winter, foxy-red in summer. Barks when alarmed. In woodlands.

► **Red Deer** *Cervus elaphus* 120–150cm high at shoulder. Large deer, rump patch yellowish-white, tail short. Coat reddish-brown in summer, greyish in winter. Usually in herds. Mainly moorlands in Britain, woodland elsewhere.

◄ **Fallow Deer** *Dama dama* 85–110cm high at shoulder. Tail with black upperside, contrasting with white rump which has black border. Summer coat is orange-brown with white spots, greyer in winter. Usually in herds. Woodland and parks.

► **Sika Deer** *Cervus nippon* 80–85cm high at shoulder. No black on upperside of tail so whole rump appears white with black upper border. Male (stag) whistles in mating season to attract females (hinds). Coat is red-brown spotted in summer, grey in winter. Woods. Not common in Britain.

▶ **Elk** *Alces alces* 150–210cm high at shoulder. Long, heavy, down curved nose. Humped shoulders. Antlers sharp and flat with many sharp points. Coat grey-brown or blackish. Flap of skin on throat. Open woodland with lakes and swamps. Not in Britain.

◀ **Wild Boar** *Sus scrofa* Body 110–150cm, tail 15–20cm. Only pig-like wild mammal in Europe. Male (boar) has large tusks and is solitary. Females (sows) usually in herds. Woods. Not in Britain.

◀ **Wild Goat** *Capra hircus* 65–85cm high at shoulder. Small and shaggy compared to domestic goat. Various colours. Both sexes horned. Hilly areas.

▶ **Mouflon** *Ovis musimon* 65–75cm high at shoulder. Like small sheep with semi-circular curving horns, smaller or absent in female. Coat hairy, reddish-brown in summer, darker in winter with white patch on sides. Hilly areas. Not in Britain.

17

Bats

▶ **Pipistrelle** *Pipistrellus pipistrellus* Body 3–5cm, wingspan 19–25cm. Brown or black, with jerky, fast flight. Smallest and commonest European bat.

◀ **Natterer's Bat** *Myotis nattereri* Body 4–5cm, wingspan 25–30cm. Brown above, white below, looking pale in flight. Long rounded ears.

▼ **Daubenton's Bat** *Myotis daubentoni* Body 4–5cm, wingspan 23–27cm. Ears short, pointed tips. Usually flies over water, early in the evening.

◀ **Greater Horseshoe Bat** *Rhinolophus ferrumequinum* Body 6–7cm, wingspan 34–39cm. Nose has horseshoe-like folds. Flies low over ground.

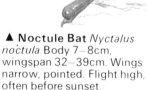

▲ **Noctule Bat** *Nyctalus noctula* Body 7–8cm, wingspan 32–39cm. Wings narrow, pointed. Flight high, often before sunset.

▲ **Long-eared Bat** *Plecotus auritus* Body 4–5cm, wingspan 23–28cm. Large, long, rabbit-shaped ears are distinctive

◀ **Whiskered Bat** *Myotis mystacinus* Body 3–5cm, wingspan 21–24cm. Small bat with narrow wings. Flight fluttering, usually near trees, early in evening.

Seals, Porpoise and Dolphin

▶ Common Seal
Phoca vitulina 130–160cm. Head puppy-like, small with short snout. Body grey or brown with spots. Usually seen swimming, or lying on sand or mud banks. The commonest seal in most parts of NW Europe, found mainly in sheltered bays and estuaries.

◀ Grey Seal *Halichoerus grypus* 195–330cm. Snout blunt. Body colour black, fawn or grey with large spots. Male much larger, darker, with thick neck. Usually seen swimming, or lying on rocks. Locally common, especially on rocky coasts.

▲ Common Porpoise *Phocaena phocaena* Up to 200cm. Swims in 'schools', rounded back shows above water. Single fin is triangular. Head short, snout blunt. Colour black, white below. All coasts round Britain.

▼ Common Dolphin *Delphinus delphis* 150–250cm. Swims in 'schools', fast moving, often leaping clear of water. Single fin points and curves towards tail. Head with distinct forehead.

19

Birds

Crest
Nape
Back
Wing
Rump
Tail
Legs
Feet

Forehead
Beak or bill
Chin or bib
Throat
Neck
Breast
Side
Wingbars
Flank

♂ Chaffinch

Birds are distinguished from all other animals by the possession of feathers. Their front limbs are in the form of wings, and most birds can fly. A bird is structured in such a way that it can do this as efficiently as possible. The wing feathers are shaped so that maximum use can be made of air currents and the bones are honeycombed with spaces full of air. Feathers are replaced by moulting and kept in good condition by preening, using the beak and oil from special glands.

Some birds travel great distances, and may fly many kilometres north in spring to nest and south in the autumn to warmer lands. During these journeys, called migrations, they navigate using the Sun and stars and their sensitivity to the Earth's magnetic field.

Birds are divided into families and orders for classification, depending on their structure. Measurements are from head to tail.

Crow
all-purpose

Bullfinch
seed-eater

Wren
insect-eater

Curlew
probing mud

◀ In some species of bird, the males are brightly coloured, like this male redstart; the females dull. The symbols used here denote male (♂) and female (♀).

Summer   Winter

◀ Look out for the labels Summer and Winter which tell you whether an illustration is of a bird's summer or winter plumage. Here is a dotterel at different times of the year.

Young   Adult

◀ Young birds such as the robin often have different patterns and colours, especially when the adults are brightly coloured. Gulls take 2 to 3 years for the young to moult and grow adult plumage.

CLUES AND HINTS

Watching: When studying birds, spend a lot of time just watching. Only then will you learn their shape, behaviour and song, so that eventually a bird can be identified almost without thinking — a magpie hopping and jerking its long tail or the flash of white rump as a bullfinch slips into the bushes. A good pair of binoculars is important. Be quiet and patient. Never disturb nesting birds.

Song: Birdsong is an invaluable aid in identifying a bird. Learn songs and calls through recordings, as well as by listening with more experienced people.

Identification: Always make notes on the spot when you have seen a bird. As far as possible, it should be compared with something familiar and all details jotted down before consulting an identification guide.

Barn owl tearing flesh

Kingfisher fish-eater

◀ Different parts of a bird's body are adapted to the way it lives. Beaks show the greatest diversity, though birds in the same family have similar beak shapes. The shapes are adapted to the kind of food the bird eats and the way it gets its food.

Shearwater, Fulmar, Gannet, Diver and Grebes

▶ **Fulmar** *Fulmarus glacialis* 46cm. Gull-like, wings long, straight and stiff in flight. No black tips. Bill thick, short with tube-like nostrils. Nests on sea cliffs. Resident.

◀ **Manx Shearwater** *Puffinus puffinus* 36cm. Flies low over water, wings held stiffly. Nests in burrows on coast. Resident.

▼ **Great Crested Grebe** *Podiceps cristatus* 46cm. Summer: ear tufts and ruff. Winter: long white neck, white patch by eye. Breeds lakes and rivers. Often on coast. Resident.

Summer

Winter

▲ **Gannet** *Sula bassana* 91cm. Large white bird, pointed long wings, black tips. Long sharp bill. Resident.

▶ **Black-throated Diver** *Gavia arctica* 63cm. Breeds in Scotland. Resident and winter visitor on coasts.

Summer

Winter

▼ **Little Grebe** *Tachybaptus ruficollis* 25cm. Small, dumpy grebe, diving often. Freshwater. Common. Summer: chestnut cheeks and neck. Winter: brown back. Resident.

Winter

Summer

Cormorants, Heron, Bittern and Stork

Continental form

Atlantic form

▶ **Shag** *Phalacrocorax aristotelis* 76cm. Like small cormorant, but all black, no white patches. Both sexes have small crest in summer. Breeds sea cliffs, not seen inland. Resident.

▲ **Cormorant** *Phalacrocorax carbo* 91cm. Large black bird, long neck and hooked bill. Breeds sea cliffs, sometimes seen inland. Resident.

▶ **Bittern** *Botaurus stellaris* 76cm. Seldom seen. Distinctive 'booming' call in summer. Stands motionless at edge of reed beds, often bill pointing upwards. Breeds in reed beds. Resident and visitor.

◀ **Heron** *Ardea cinerea* 91cm. Very large grey bird with long neck, legs and bill. Broad wings, trailing legs and neck folded back in flight, with slow, flapping wing beats. Resident.

▶ **White Stork** *Ciconia ciconia* 102cm. Very large white bird with red legs and bill. Wings with black edges. Nests on or near houses. Not in Britain.

23

Ducks

◄ **Mallard** *Anas platyrhynchos* 58cm. Male has green head, chestnut breast. Female brown with blue/purple speculum; the male is similar when it moults (August). Large numbers on coast in winter. Common. Resident.

▶ **Teal** *Anas crecca* 36cm. Small, agile duck. Male has chestnut head, green eye patch. Back and sides grey, long white stripe down side. Female brown, speculum green. Male call, a musical whistle. Flight rapid. Flocks in winter. Upends when feeding. Resident.

◄ **Wigeon** *Anas penelope* 46cm. Male has chestnut head with creamy-white centre. White line on side, black and white near tail. Female brown, bill blue. Male call is double whistle. Winter visitor to coast and lakes.

▶▼ **Pintail** *Anas acuta* 63cm. Male has long pointed tail, brown head, long white neck with white 'finger' behind eye. Black and white near tail. Female brown, shorter, pointed tail, long neck, blue-grey bill. A few breed but mainly winter visitor in small numbers.

▲ Shoveler *Anas clypeata* 51cm.
Both sexes have large, heavy,
spoon-shaped bill and low
forehead. Dabbles for food on
lakes and ponds. Resident and
winter visitor.

▼ Tufted Duck
Aythya fuligula 43cm.
Male is black with
white sides and tuft at
back of head. Female
dark brown, paler sides,
small tuft. Feeds by
diving. Resident and
winter visitor.

◀ Pochard *Aythya ferina* 46cm.
Male has red head, black breast.
Female brown, blue band on bill.
Dives to feed. Resident and
winter visitor.

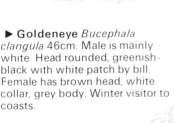

▶ Goldeneye *Bucephala
clangula* 46cm. Male is mainly
white. Head rounded, greenish-
black with white patch by bill.
Female has brown head, white
collar, grey body. Winter visitor to
coasts.

◀ Common Scoter
Melanitta nigra 51cm. Male is
black with rounded back and
heavy head. Bill yellow with
large knob at base. Female
brown, pale cheeks and neck.
Winter visitor to coasts.

Ducks

◀ **Eider Duck** *Somateria mollissima* 61cm. Heavy, triangular-shaped head, broad flat bill. Male is black and white. Female brown with dark bars. Winter visitor and resident.

▼ **Red-breasted Merganser** *Mergus serrator* 56cm. Male has long red bill, green crested head, red breast. Female brown. Winter visitor and resident.

▶ **Goosander** *Mergus merganser* 66cm. Male is large with long red bill, green head, pink sides. Female has brown head, distinct throat patch. Winters on fresh water.

◀ **Smew** *Mergus albellus* 41cm. Male is dumpy, black and white with crest and slender bill. Female has chestnut head, white cheeks. Lakes and rivers, sometimes coasts. Winter visitor.

▶ **Shelduck** *Tadorna tadorna* 61cm. Male and female similar, but male has knob on red bill. Flight slower than other ducks. Breeds on coasts. Resident.

Geese and Swans

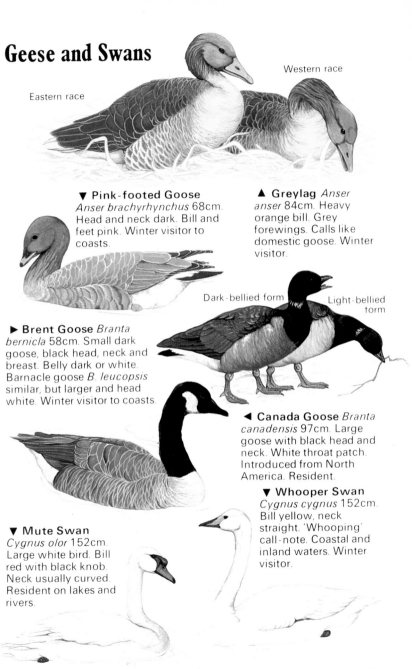

Eastern race

Western race

▼ Pink-footed Goose
Anser brachyrhynchus 68cm.
Head and neck dark. Bill and
feet pink. Winter visitor to
coasts.

▲ Greylag *Anser
anser* 84cm. Heavy
orange bill. Grey
forewings. Calls like
domestic goose. Winter
visitor.

Dark-bellied form

Light-bellied
form

► Brent Goose *Branta
bernicla* 58cm. Small dark
goose, black head, neck and
breast. Belly dark or white.
Barnacle goose *B. leucopsis*
similar, but larger and head
white. Winter visitor to coasts.

◄ Canada Goose *Branta
canadensis* 97cm. Large
goose with black head and
neck. White throat patch.
Introduced from North
America. Resident.

▼ Whooper Swan
Cygnus cygnus 152cm.
Bill yellow, neck
straight. 'Whooping'
call-note. Coastal and
inland waters. Winter
visitor.

▼ Mute Swan
Cygnus olor 152cm.
Large white bird. Bill
red with black knob.
Neck usually curved.
Resident on lakes and
rivers.

Birds of Prey

Light form

Dark form

◄ **Buzzard** *Buteo buteo* 53cm. Both sexes various shades of brown. Barred tail. Circles with little wing flapping. Resident.

► **Golden Eagle** *Aquila chrysaetos* 84cm. Both sexes brown, adult has golden head. Tail square. Heavy head visible in flight. Resident in mountains of northern Britain.

◄ **Goshawk** *Accipiter gentilis* 53cm. Rounded wings, barred underparts, long tail. Female larger than male. Flies fast and low when hunting. Few breed in woodland. Resident.

▼ **Sparrowhawk** *Accipiter nisus* 33cm. Male grey above, barred reddish breast. Female larger, brown, barred breast. Flight fast and low when hunting. Woodland. Common. Resident.

▼ **Marsh Harrier** *Circus aeruginosus* 51cm. Large hawk with broad wings seen flying low over marshes. Male has long grey tail and wings. Female dark with pale head and throat. Wanders in winter.

▼ **Hen Harrier** *Circus cyaneus* 46cm. Male is grey above, long narrow wings, long tail. Female brown, white rump. Moorland. Wanders in winter.

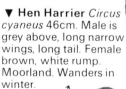

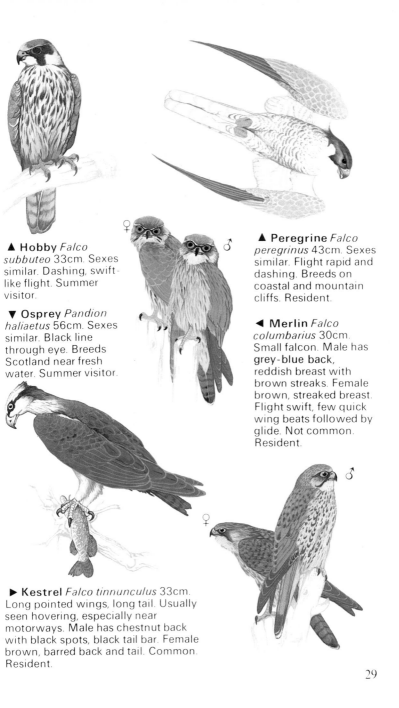

▲ **Hobby** *Falco subbuteo* 33cm. Sexes similar. Dashing, swift-like flight. Summer visitor.

▼ **Osprey** *Pandion haliaetus* 56cm. Sexes similar. Black line through eye. Breeds Scotland near fresh water. Summer visitor.

▲ **Peregrine** *Falco peregrinus* 43cm. Sexes similar. Flight rapid and dashing. Breeds on coastal and mountain cliffs. Resident.

◄ **Merlin** *Falco columbarius* 30cm. Small falcon. Male has grey-blue back, reddish breast with brown streaks. Female brown, streaked breast. Flight swift, few quick wing beats followed by glide. Not common. Resident.

► **Kestrel** *Falco tinnunculus* 33cm. Long pointed wings, long tail. Usually seen hovering, especially near motorways. Male has chestnut back with black spots, black tail bar. Female brown, barred back and tail. Common. Resident.

29

Game Birds

▶ **Red Grouse** *Lagopus lagopus scoticus* 38cm. Both sexes red-brown, darker wings and tail. Red wattle over eye. Wings down, curved when gliding. Breeds moorland. Resident.

▼ **Willow Grouse** *Lagopus lagopus* 38cm. Similar to ptarmigan but at lower altitudes. Male has brown back in summer. Female as ptarmigan. Turns white in winter, no black on head. Not in Britain.

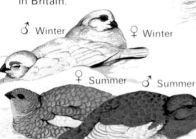

♂ Winter ♀ Winter

♀ Summer ♂ Summer

▲ **Black Grouse** *Lyrurus tetrix* 53cm. Male is blue-black with red wattles, curved, forked tail. Female brown, barred feathers. Breeds moorland. Resident.

▼ **Capercaillie** *Tetrao urogallus* 86cm. Turkey-sized game bird. Male dark grey, red wattles. Female brown, barred feathers. Woodlands in Scotland. Resident.

▼ **Ptarmigan** *Lagopus mutus* 36cm. Summer: white wings, male body grey, female brown. Winter: all white. Mountains of Scotland. Resident.

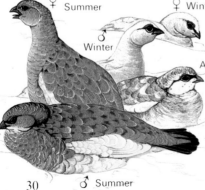

♀ Summer
♀ Winter
♂ Winter
Autumn

♂ Summer

► **Hazelhen** *Tetrastes bonasia* 36cm. Small brown game bird. Both sexes have round, grey tail with black band. Short crest on head. Male has black throat, white border. Not in Britain.

▲ **Quail** *Coturnix coturnix* 18cm. Very small, dumpy game bird. Sandy-brown with darker streaks. Shy, but can be heard calling in grass or corn. Summer visitor.

► **Partridge** *Perdix perdix* 30cm. Round, dumpy, brown game bird with chestnut head, reddish tail, grey neck. Male chestnut, horseshoe-shaped mark on breast, paler or absent in females. Farmland. Resident.

◄ **Pheasant** *Phasianus colchicus* Male 84cm, long tail, green head, reddish-brown back and breast. Female 58cm, brown. Call 'kok-kok'. Resident.

31

Crane, Rails and Crakes

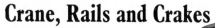

▼ **Moorhen** *Gallinula chloropus*
33cm. Red forehead and bill,
brown back, dark-blue breast,
white stripe along side, white
patch by tail. Near water. Resident.

▼ **Crane** *Grus grus*
114cm. Large heron-
like bird. Long neck and
legs. Head and neck
black with long white
stripe, body grey. Long
black, drooping 'tail'
feathers. Not in Britain.

▲ **Coot** *Fulica atra* 38cm. Both sexes
black with broad white forehead. Back
rounded. Large ponds and lakes.
Resident.

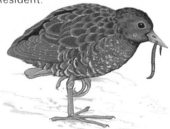

▲ **Spotted Crake**
Porzana porzana 23cm.
Small brown bird,
streaked and spotted
with white, barred
sides. Jerks tail when
anxious. Swamps and
wet places. Winter
visitor.

▲ **Water Rail** *Rallus
aquaticus* 28cm. Long,
slender, red bill with
black tip. Black and
white barred flanks.
Resident.

▶ **Corncrake** *Crex
crex* 25cm. Small
thrush-sized brown
bird, chestnut on wings.
Summer visitor.

Waders

◄ Oystercatcher
Haematopus ostralegus
43cm. Long orange bill,
pinkish legs. Breeds coasts
and estuaries. Sometimes
inland. Resident.

▼ Golden Plover *Pluvialis*
pricaria 28cm In summer,
[bl]ack spangled black and gold.
[B]reeds moorland. Note liquid
[w]histle. Resident

Southern form
Summer

Northern form
Summer

Winter

▼ Ringed Plover *Charadrius*
hiaticula 19cm. Resident. **Little**
Ringed Plover *Charadrius dubius*
15cm. Small, active birds, pointed
wings. Inland. Summer visitor.

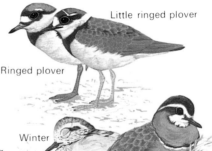

Little ringed plover

Ringed plover

Winter

Summer

► Dotterel *Eudromias*
morinellus 23cm. Summer: white
eye stripe, white band dividing
chestnut belly from grey breast.
Winter: underparts duller. No wing
bar in flight. Summer visitor.

◄ Lapwing *Vanellus*
vanellus 30cm. Long
crest. Calls 'pee wit'.
Breeds moors, fields.
Resident.

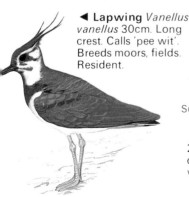

Winter

Summer

▲ Turnstone *Arenaria interpres*
23cm. Patchy appearance in summer,
orange legs. Rocky shores. Winter
visitor.

33

Waders

▶ **Curlew** *Numenius arquata* 56cm. Large brown bird with long, down-curved bill, long legs. Call note, distinctive liquid whistle. Spring song, musical bubbling notes. Breeds moorland. Large flocks on coast in winter. Resident.

▼ **Snipe** *Gallinago gallinago* 27cm. Rich red-brown bird, long bill, barred tail, pointed wings, striped head. Harsh call when disturbed. Wet places. Resident

▲ **Woodcock** *Scolopax rusticola* 36cm. Head round, barred. Rich red-brown plumage, belly finely striped. Rounded wings. Resident.

▼ **Common Sandpiper** *Tringa hypoleucos* 20cm. Dumpy brown bird, white below, always bobbing up and down. Breeds near fresh water. Summer visitor.

▼ **Black-tailed Godwit** *Limosa limosa* 41cm. Long straight bill. Few breed in Britain, marshy places. On coast in spring and autumn. Passage migrant.

▼ **Bar-tailed Godwit** *Limosa lapponica* 38cm. Similar to black-tailed godwit, but bill turned upward. In flight no wing bar, tail barred and feet hardly show. Passage migrant.

Summer

Winter

Winter

Summer

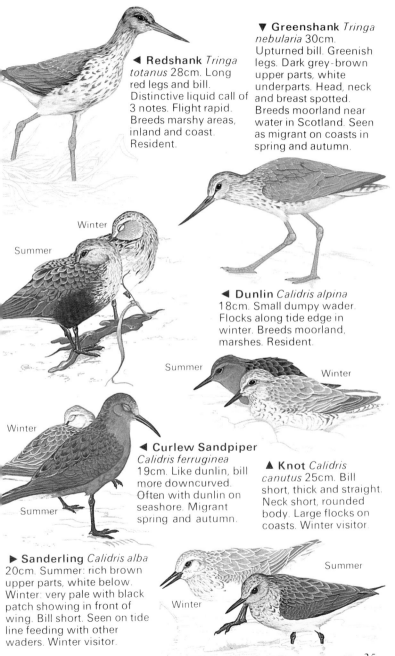

◀ **Redshank** *Tringa totanus* 28cm. Long red legs and bill. Distinctive liquid call of 3 notes. Flight rapid. Breeds marshy areas, inland and coast. Resident.

▼ **Greenshank** *Tringa nebularia* 30cm. Upturned bill. Greenish legs. Dark grey-brown upper parts, white underparts. Head, neck and breast spotted. Breeds moorland near water in Scotland. Seen as migrant on coasts in spring and autumn.

Winter

Summer

◀ **Dunlin** *Calidris alpina* 18cm. Small dumpy wader. Flocks along tide edge in winter. Breeds moorland, marshes. Resident.

Summer

Winter

Winter

◀ **Curlew Sandpiper** *Calidris ferruginea* 19cm. Like dunlin, bill more downcurved. Often with dunlin on seashore. Migrant spring and autumn.

▲ **Knot** *Calidris canutus* 25cm. Bill short, thick and straight. Neck short, rounded body. Large flocks on coasts. Winter visitor.

Summer

▶ **Sanderling** *Calidris alba* 20cm. Summer: rich brown upper parts, white below. Winter: very pale with black patch showing in front of wing. Bill short. Seen on tide line feeding with other waders. Winter visitor.

Summer

Winter

35

Waders

◀ **Avocet** *Recurvirostra avosetta* 43cm. Long thin, upturned bill. Black and white plumage, long slate-blue legs. Shows black and white pattern in flight. Feeds by moving head from side to side in shallow water. Summer visitor, migrant.

▼ **Ruff** *Philomachus pugnax* 30cm. Male is unmistakable in summer — large ruff of feathers on neck which varies in colour. Passage migrant in spring and autumn.

♂ Winter   ♀   ♂ Summer

♂ Summer

▲ **Black-winged Stilt** *Himantopus himantopus* 38cm. Very long red legs, straight black bill. Male has black back with white underparts. Female brown back. In flight, dark pointed wings contrast with white body. Rare visitor.

♀   ♂ Winter

◀ **Stone Curlew** *Burhinus oedicnemus* 41cm. Bill short, gull-like. Large yellow eye. Rounded head. Colour sandy-brown with darker streaks. Heathland, open woodland. Summer visitor.

Gulls

▶ **Black-headed Gull**
Larus ridibundus 38cm.
Small gull. Inland and
coasts. Nests in
colonies. The similar
Mediterranean gull *L.
melanocephalus* has no
black on wing. The little
gull *L. minutus* is very
small. Resident.

Mediterranean gull in winter

Little gull in winter

Black-headed gull in winter

▼ **Lesser Black-backed
Gull** *Larus fuscus* 53cm. Bill
yellow, red spot. Legs yellow,
slate-grey upper parts. Wing
has black tips, spotted white.
Nests at seashore. Summer
visitor.

British form

Scandinavian form

▼ **Great Black-
backed Gull** *Larus
marinus* 68cm. The
largest gull. Legs pink.
Bill heavy, yellow with
red spot. Chiefly on
coasts but also inland.
Resident.

▼ **Herring Gull** *Larus argentatus*
56cm. Legs flesh-coloured. Back and
wings grey. Bill yellow, red spot.
Laughing cry. Coasts and inland. Nests
in colonies. Resident.

◀ **Common Gull**
Larus canus 41cm. Legs
and bill greenish. Back
and wings grey, wing
tips black with white
spots. Often inland as
well as on coast.
Resident.

37

Gulls and Terns

▶ **Kittiwake** *Rissa tridactyla*
41cm. Yellow bill (no marks),
large eye. Dark legs, dove-grey
back. Wing tips black, no white
spots. Call 'kit-i-wake'. Nests in
colonies.

◀ **Black Tern** *Chlidonias niger*
24cm. Bill black, legs red, white
under tail, pointed wings. Tail
forked. Flight is butterfly-like over
reeds and marshes. Passage
migrant.

▶ **Common Tern** *Sterna hirundo*
36cm. Long pointed wings,
forked tail, red bill with black tip.
Head black, back grey. Flight
bouncy, often diving into sea to
fish. Harsh single call note.
Coasts. Also inland. Summer
visitor.

▶ **Sandwich Tern**
Sterna sandvicensis
41cm. Large tern.
Heavy black bill with
yellow tip. Forked tail.
Black head, feathers
forming crest at back.
Legs black. Harsh
rasping call distinctive.
Coastal. Summer
visitor.

◀ **Little Tern** *Sterna albifrons*
24cm. Smallest tern. Yellow bill
with black tip, legs yellow. Tail
forked. Sandy coasts and shingle.
Summer visitor.

Auks

◀ **Guillemot** *Uria aalge* 41cm. Bill straight, slender, long. Neck slender. White line on wing. Flight whirring on small, narrow, rapidly beating wings. Low over water. Nests in colonies on sea cliffs. Resident.

Summer

Winter

Summer

▶ **Puffin** *Fratercula arctica* 30cm. Small auk with large beak, flattened sideways. In summer brightly coloured, red, blue and yellow; less noticeable in winter. Legs orange. Nests in burrows on coasts and islands. Carries many fish at a time in beak. Resident.

Winter

Summer

◀ **Razorbill** *Alca torda* 41cm. Very like guillemot but bill short, deep and heavy looking, with white mark across it. Nests in colonies on sea cliffs with guillemots. Resident.

Winter

39

Pigeon, Doves and Cuckoo

▶ **Stock Dove**
Columba oenas 33cm.
Like small woodpigeon.
No white on wings or
neck. Two narrow
black wingbars. Rump
grey. Woodland.
Resident.

◀ **Woodpigeon**
Columba palumbus
41cm. Largest pigeon.
White on neck and
broad white mark on
wings. Resident.

▼ **Rock Dove**
Columba livia 33cm.
Two broad black bands
across wings. Rump
white. Ancestor of
domestic pigeon.
Resident.

◀ **Turtle Dove**
Streptopelia turtur
28cm. Slender pigeon
with rounded tail.
Fields, small woods.
Summer visitor.

◀ **Collared Dove**
Streptopelia decaocto
30cm. Slender, buff-
coloured dove, distinct
black patch on neck.
Towns and villages.
Resident.

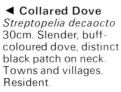

▶ **Cuckoo** *Cuculus canorus*
33cm. Male call is well-
known 'cuckoo'. Blue-grey
back, barred breast. Female
brown, lays single egg in nests
of other birds. Young cuckoo
ejects young and is reared by
its foster parents. Summer
visitor.

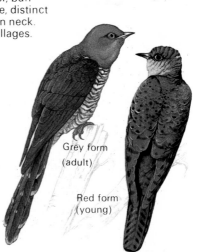

Grey form
(adult)

Red form
(young)

40

Owls

Light-breasted form

Dark-breasted form

▶ **Barn Owl** *Tyto alba* 36cm. Long rounded wings, large round head. Upper parts golden brown with black spots. Flies silently at dusk. Near buildings. Resident.

◀ **Eagle Owl** *Bubo bubo* 68cm. Very large owl. Long ear tufts, large orange eyes. Brown with boldly streaked breast. Rare in Britain.

▼ **Pygmy Owl** *Glaucidium passerinum* 18cm. Small owl. Active by day. Not in Britain.

own form   Grey form

▶ **Little Owl** *Athene noctua* 23cm. Broad head with yellow eyes. Brown back with large white spots. Active by day. Open country. Resident.

◀ **Tawny Owl** *Strix aluco* 38cm. Brown or grey-brown owl with heavily streaked plumage. Large head and black eyes, no ear tufts. Active at night. Voice is the familiar hoot. Wooded areas. Resident.

◀ **Long-eared Owl** *Asio otus* 36cm. Long ear tufts, orange eyes, body slimmer than tawny owl. Colour similar. Active at night. Chiefly in coniferous woods. Resident.

▶ **Short-eared Owl** *Asio flammeus* 38cm. Hunts by day. Usually seen flying low, on long wings. Moors, open country. Resident.

41

Nightjar, Swift, Kingfisher and Related Birds

▶ **Nightjar** *Caprimulgus europaeus* 28cm. Moth-like flight at dusk. Long wings and tail. Open woods. Summer visitor.

◀ **Swift** *Apus apus* 16cm. Usually seen in flight. Dark with long, curved, pointed wings which flicker rapidly. Tail forked. Screams in flight, especially in the evening. Summer visitor.

◀ **Kingfisher** *Alcedo atthis* 16cm. Brightly-coloured bird with large head, long pointed bill. Flies low and very fast. Fresh water. Resident.

▼ **Roller** *Coracias garrulus* 30cm. Like small jay in size. Chestnut back, blue-green underparts unmistakable both in flight and on ground. Rare in Britain.

Crest up

Crest down

▲ **Bee-eater** *Merops apiaster* 28cm. Curved bill, brilliant colours. Rare summer visitor.

▶ **Hoopoe** *Upupa epops* 28cm. Long crest, tipped with black, long curved bill. Buff-pink head and breast. Rare in Britain.

Woodpeckers

▶ **Black Woodpecker**
Dryocopus martius 46cm. All
black woodpecker with
crimson crown, yellow eyes
and pale yellow bill. Large
bird. Coniferous forest, not
Britain.

▼ **Wryneck** *Jynx torquilla*
16cm. Not often seen. Grey-
brown with upper parts
mottled and streaked,
underparts barred. Small bill,
tail barred. Summer visitor.

▶ **Grey-headed
Woodpecker** *Picus canus*
25cm. Similar to green
woodpecker but smaller with
grey head and neck. Not in
Britain.

▶ **Green Woodpecker**
Picus viridis 30cm. Large,
jackdaw-sized woodpecker.
Dark green upper parts, red
crown, yellow rump. Often
heard, when laughing cry
is easily recognized.
Flight up and down, with
wings closing every few
beats; long bill, short tail
noticeable. Often feeds on
ground. Deciduous woodland
with old trees. Resident.

43

Woodpeckers

▶ **Great Spotted Woodpecker**
Dendrocopos major
23cm. Black and white with large, white shoulder patches and crimson underneath tail. Male has crimson patch on head. All kinds of woodland. Resident.

◀ **Middle Spotted Woodpecker** *Dendrocopos medius* 20cm. Cheeks white, crown crimson. Woodland. Not in Britain.

▼ **White-backed Woodpecker** *Dendrocop[leucotos* 25cm. Similar in colour to great spotted woodpecker. No white shoulder patch, lower bac[white. Not in Britain.

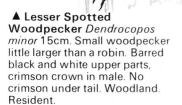

▲ **Lesser Spotted Woodpecker** *Dendrocopos minor* 15cm. Small woodpecker little larger than a robin. Barred black and white upper parts, crimson crown in male. No crimson under tail. Woodland. Resident.

Larks, Martins and Swallows

▶ **Skylark** *Alauda arvensis* 18cm. Small crest, long tail with white outer tail feathers. Distinctive continuous song as bird rises and then descends with open wings. Resident

▼ **Woodlark** *Lullula arborea* 15cm. Tail short, distinct white eye stripe meeting at back of head. Open woodland.

▲ **Crested Lark** *Galerida cristata* 16cm. Distinct, long crest. Buff, not white, outer tail feathers, tail short. Rare visitor.

▼ **House Martin** *Delichon urbica* 13cm. White rump and underparts, upper parts blue. No breast band. Tail short with slight fork. Usually near buildings. Summer visitor.

▼ **Sand Martin** *Riparia riparia* 13cm. White breast has brown band across. Upper parts and wings brown. Usually seen flying near water. Summer visitor.

▲ **Swallow** *Hirundo rustica* 19cm. Long tail streamers in adult. Long wings, blue neck-band, red throat with buffish-white underparts, wings pointed. Flight wheeling and circling. Summer visitor.

Crows

◀ **Raven** *Corvus corax* 63cm. The largest crow. All black, bill heavy, stout. Easily distinguished by 'croaking' note. In flight, tail is wedge-shaped. Often soars and tumbles in flight. Hills and coastal cliffs. Resident.

▶ **Carrion Crow** *Corvus corone corone* 46cm. Bill thicker and heavier than rook, no bare patch at base of bill. Distinctive harsh call. Usually in pairs. Resident.

◀ **Hooded Crow** *Corvus corone cornix* 46cm. Like carrion crow, but has grey back and underparts. Closely related, often interbreed. Resident.

▶ **Jackdaw** *Corvus monedula* 33cm. Small crow. Grey nape, short bill. Call 'jack jack' distinctive. Often with rooks. Usually in small groups, even when nesting. Flies more rapidly than other crows. Resident.

◀ **Rook** *Corvus frugilegus* 46cm. Black crow with bare patch of skin at base of bill. Feathers at top of leg loose and 'baggy'. Usually in flocks, nesting in colonies. Farmland. Resident.

Crows and Oriole

▲ **Jay** *Garrulus glandarius* 36cm. White rump and black tail easily seen in jerky flight. Bright blue and black on wings, pinkish-brown body. Harsh call. Resident.

▲ **Magpie** *Pica pica* 46cm. Distinctive black and white plumage. Long wedge-shaped tail. Usually hops, but can walk. Chattering call. Open country with hedges, open woodland. Resident.

▶ **Chough** *Pyrrhocorax pyrrhocorax* 38cm. Like large slender jackdaw with bright red, long, downward-curved bill and red legs. Flies with the feathers at tips of rounded wings well separated, soaring and diving with ease. Coastal and inland cliffs. Resident.

◀ **Golden Oriole** *Oriolus oriolus* 24cm. Thrush-sized, bright yellow body contrasting with black wings and tail make male bird unmistakable. Female and young greenish-yellow with dark wings and tail. Distinctive musical whistle. Rare summer visitor.

Tits

◄ Blue Tit *Parus caeruleus* 11cm. White cheeks with line through eye. Active and agile. Flight weak, fluttering. Gardens and woodland. Resident.

▲ Great Tit *Parus major* 14cm. The largest tit, underparts yellow with black streak down centre, cheek patches white on black head. Often feeds upside down. Resident.

► Marsh Tit *Parus palustris* 11cm. Glossy black cap and black chin on otherwise brown tit, darker above, paler below. Double harsh call note. Woods and copses. Resident.

► Willow Tit *Parus montanus* (far right) 11cm. Similar, dull not glossy crown and light patch on side of wing. Damp woodland.

Southern form

Northern form

▲ Coal Tit *Parus ater* 11cm. Black head with white patch at back of neck, whitish cheeks, black throat. Double white wingbar. Woodland, especially conifers. Resident.

► Long-tailed Tit *Aegithalos caudatus* 14cm. Very long narrow tail. White crown bordered with black. Black and white colouring unlike other tits. Woodland, hedges. Resident.

Babbler, Nuthatch, Creeper, Wren and Dipper

▶ **Bearded Tit** *Panurus biarmicus* 16cm. It is the only species of babbler found in Europe. Both sexes have long brown tail and upper parts. Male has black stripe by bill and grey head, black under tail. Flight slow, with trailing tail. Resident.

▶ **Tree Creeper** *Certhia familiaris* 14cm. Small brown bird with curved bill, white underparts. Usually seen 'jerking' up tree trunk, supported by tail. Woodlands. Resident.

Treecreeper

Short-toed treecreeper

▲ **Nuthatch** *Sitta europaea* 14cm. Large head and bill, short tail, slate-blue upper parts, black line through eye, buff orange underparts. Woodlands. Resident.

◀ **Wren** *Troglodytes troglodytes* 10cm. Tiny, stumpy, dark brown with short, cocked tail. Flight short, with whirring wings. Woods and gardens. Resident.

▶ **Dipper** *Cinclus cinclus* 18cm. A plump, thrush-sized brown bird with a white throat and short tail. Always by running water, bobs up and down on stones. Resident.

49

Thrushes, Chats and Redstarts

▶ **Song Thrush** *Turdus philomelos*
23cm. Brown bird with buff, spotted
breast. Eye large, dark. Hops, cocking
head to one side. Cracks snails on
stones. Gardens. Resident.

▲ **Redwing** *Turdus iliacus*
20cm. Broad white eye stripe,
red patch on flanks, dark
brown back. Fields. Winter
visitor.

▲ **Mistle Thrush** *Turdus
viscivorus* 28cm. Larger, greyer
bird than song thrush, white tips
to tail feathers, underside of wing
pale in flight. Resident.

▲ **Fieldfare** *Turdus
pilaris* 25cm. Grey head
and chestnut back.
Pale grey rump, black
tail in flight. Winter
visitor.

▶ **Blackbird** *Turdus
merula* 25cm. Male all
black, yellow bill.
Female dark brown.
Chattering call.
Gardens, woods.
Resident.

◀ **Wheatear**
Oenanthe oenanthe
15cm. Both sexes have
white rump, easily seen
in flight. Male is blue-
grey with black tail and
wings. Heaths and
hillsides. Summer
resident.

► Black Redstart
Phoenicurus ochruros 14cm.
Both sexes have red rump and tail. Tail flicked constantly. Summer visitor and migrant.

▲ Nightingale
Luscinia megarhynchos 16cm. Shy bird usually discovered by liquid song. All brown, no markings. Woods and thickets. Summer visitor.

▼ Bluethroat
Luscinia svecica 14cm. Robin-like with blue throat. Flicks tail. Rare in Britain.

► Stonechat *Saxicola torquata* 13cm. Usually seen on gorse bush or bracken, flicking wings and tail with clicking call. Commons, hillsides. Resident.

♂ White-spotted form

♂ Red-spotted form

▼ Robin *Erithacus rubecula* 14cm. Red breast with pale grey border, brown back. Gardens, woodlands. Resident.

► Whinchat *Saxicola rubetra* 13cm. Both sexes have eye stripe, white in male, buff in female. Moors, heaths. Summer visitor.

► Redstart
Phoenicurus phoenicurus 14cm. Both sexes have chestnut tail which is always quivering. Gardens, open woodland, hillsides. Summer visitor.

51

Warblers

▼ **Sedge Warbler** *Acrocephalus schoenobaenus* 13cm. Brown bird, broad white eye stripe and streaked back. Not often seen. Chattering song.

▲ **Reed Warbler** *Acrocephalus scirpaceus* 13cm. Brown bird, no streaks on back. Reed beds, long grass near water. Summer resident.

◄ **Blackcap** *Sylvia atricapilla* 14cm. Keeps to tree tops, singing its sweet liquid song. Male grey-brown with black cap. Female brown, with red-brown cap. Summer visitor.

► **Garden Warbler** *Sylvia borin* 14cm. Brown bird, paler below, with no markings. Shy, like blackcap. Song similar but more hurried. Prefers woodland with more undergrowth than blackcap. Summer visitor.

Warblers and Goldcrest

♂ ♀

▼ Dartford Warbler
Sylvia undata 13cm.
Dark bird with long
tail, often cocked
upwards. Heaths.
Resident.

▲ Whitethroat *Sylvia
communis* 14cm. White
throat, reddish-brown on
wings, white outer tail
feathers in both sexes. Song,
rapid chatter. Hedges and
thickets. Summer visitor.

▶ Willow Warbler
Phylloscopus trochilus 11cm.
Brownish-yellow warbler, pale
brown legs. Song, descending
liquid notes. Feeds in tree tops.
Summer visitor.

▼ Wood Warbler
Phylloscopus sibilatrix
13cm. Yellow breast
and eye stripe.
Woodland. Summer
visitor.

▲ Chiffchaff
Phylloscopus collybita
11cm. Brownish-
yellow warbler with
black legs. Song
'chiffchaff' repeated.
Woodland. Summer
visitor.

♀

♂

◀ Goldcrest *Regulus regulus* 9cm.
Very small, plump, greenish bird with
white wingbars and gold crown
between black stripes. Woodland.
Resident.

53

Flycatchers, Dunnock and Pipits

◄ **Pied Flycatcher** *Ficedula hypoleuca* 13cm. White wing patch, white on side of tail. Catches insects. Summer visitor.

► **Spotted Flycatcher** *Muscicapa striata* 14cm. Makes short flights to catch insects. Summer visitor.

♂ Summer

► **Dunnock** *Prunella modularis* 15cm. Often seen creeping mouse-like through undergrowth. Robin-like, but grey breast. Brown, streaked back. Resident.

▼ **Meadow Pipit** *Anthus pratensis* 15cm. Like small, slender skylark, no crest. Open country and moorland. Resident.

► **Tree Pipit** *Anthus trivialis* 15cm. Very similar to meadow pipit but warmer brown. Distinctive song, delivered on outstretched wings, trills followed by single notes. Open woodland. Summer visitor.

► **Rock Pipit** *Anthus spinoletta* 16cm. Much darker brown than meadow pipit, with dark legs and greyish, not white, outer tail feathers. Usually found on rocky sea shores. Resident.

Wagtails, Waxwing, Shrikes and Starling

▼ **Pied Wagtail** *Motacilla alba* 18cm. Long tail, always moving up and down. Runs quickly. Black and white pattern unmistakeable. Open country, often near water. Resident.

Winter

ummer

▼ **Grey Wagtail** *Motacilla cinerea* 18cm. Bright yellow underparts. Male has black throat in summer. Usually near water. Resident.

♂ Summer

◀ **Waxwing** *Bombycilla garrulus* 18cm. Pinkish-buff plumage, long crest, short, yellow-tipped tail. Small flocks, feed on berries. Winter visitor.

▼ **Red-backed Shrike** *Lanius collurio* 18cm. Hooked beak, no white on wings but patches on tail. Commons, open woodland with thickets. Summer visitor.

◀ **Great Grey Shrike** *Lanius excubitor* 24cm. A thrush-sized bird, hooked bill, grey back. Winter visitor.

♂   ♀

Winter

▶ **Starling** *Sturnus vulgaris* 21cm. Long pointed bill, yellow in summer. Short tail, glossy black feathers, speckled in winter. Resident.

Summer

55

Finches

◀ **Greenfinch** *Carduelis chloris*
15cm. Flight up and down showing
pattern of yellow and green. Gardens,
open areas. Resident.

▼ **Hawfinch** *Coccothraustes
coccothraustes* 18cm. Large finch
with thick bill. Short tail, broad white
patches on wings. Call note, a metallic
click. Woodland. Resident.

▶ **Goldfinch**
Carduelis carduelis
13cm. Black and
yellow pattern with red
on head. Flight erratic,
often calling all the
time. Resident.

▼ **Linnet** *Acanthis
cannabina* 13cm.
Streaked, chestnut
back, white outer tail
feathers, head streaked
greyish. Bill dark.
Twitters. Resident.

▼ **Siskin** *Carduelis
spinus* 12cm. Small
finch, short forked tail.
Yellow rump, wingbar
and tail patches.
Woodland. Resident.

◄ **Redpoll** *Acanthis flammea* 13cm. Red head, black bib, no white on forked tail. Male has pink breast. Twittering call. Sings in spring, circling slowly above trees. Resident.

► **Bullfinch** *Pyrrhula pyrrhula* 15cm. Large, plump finch with conspicuous white rump, black wings and tail. Heavy bill, black cap. Male has bright red breast. Soft, piping whistle. Woodland.

♂ Summer

♂ Winter

▲ **Chaffinch** *Fringilla coelebs* 15cm. Double white wingbar, white outer tail feathers. Male slate-blue head, pink breast. Female greenish-brown. Common resident.

◄ **Crossbill** *Loxia curvirostra* 16cm. Heavy crossed bill. Short forked tail, wings and tail dark. Male is bright red, female greenish, plumage streaked. Coniferous woodland. Feeds on cones. Resident.

57

Buntings and Sparrows

► **Corn Bunting** *Emberiza calandra* 18cm. Like large sparrow, with heavy, stout bill. Pale brown with streaked plumage, no white on tail. Bill and legs yellowish. Resident.

◄ **Yellowhammer** *Emberiza citrinella* 16cm. Chestnut rump, white outer tail feathers. Male has yellow head and underparts, female browner. Open country. Resident.

► **Cirl Bunting** *Emberiza cirlus* 16cm. Olive-brown rump. Male has black throat. Stripe through eye. Resident.

◄ **Ortolan Bunting** *Emberiza hortulana* 16cm. Yellow throat, yellow ring round eye, grey head and chest. Female paler, streaked chest. Passage migrant.

► **Snow Bunting** *Plectrophenax nivalis* 16cm. White underparts, white patches on wing and tail. Male, summer: head white, back black. Winter: head brown, back brown, streaked black like female and young. On coast. Sometimes flocks in winter. Resident.

♂ Winter

♀

♂ Summer

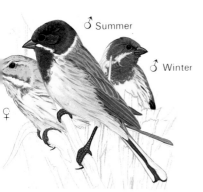

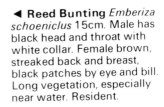

◀ Reed Bunting *Emberiza schoeniclus* 15cm. Male has black head and throat with white collar. Female brown, streaked back and breast, black patches by eye and bill. Long vegetation, especially near water. Resident.

▶ Rock Bunting *Emberiza cia* 16cm. Chestnut-red, dark wings and tail, grey head, striped crown. Female paler and duller. Outer tail feathers white. Not in Britain.

◀ House Sparrow *Passer domesticus* 15cm. Male with grey crown, whitish underparts, black throat. Female has pale eye stripe. Chirps monotonously. Found chiefly in towns and villages. Resident.

◀ Tree Sparrow *Passer montanus* 14cm. Sexes similar, more brightly coloured than house sparrow, with chestnut crown, white cheeks with black spot. Occurs more in country than house sparrow. Open woodland, hedgerows. Resident.

▶ Rock Sparrow *Petronia petronia* 14cm. Dull brown, streaked bird resembling female house sparrow, but crown has broad stripes. Yellow spot on breast. Not in Britain.

59

Amphibians and Reptiles

Amphibians and reptiles are animals which have backbones and are 'cold-blooded', which means they are unable to regulate their body temperature. Their activity depends on the temperature, so in cold weather, especially in winter, they become inactive.

Reptiles are adapted to living on land by their hard, scaly skins, which do not grow and are shed from time to time. The reptiles of northern Europe are divided into snakes and lizards. Snakes have no legs, but 'walk' on numerous ribs, the large scales on the belly stretching right across to help movement. Their jaws are hinged so that they can be opened widely to swallow large prey. Lizards have four limbs and a tail. The latter may be regrown if damaged. Most snakes and lizards lay eggs, but some, including the viper or adder and the slow-worm, produce active young. Amphibians include the frogs, toads and newts. They have soft skins, kept moist by glands and by living near water or in damp places. Eggs are laid in water and the young (tadpoles) breathe with gills and have tails. Frogs and toads have no tails as adults; newts have long tails flattened sideways.

◀ **European Tree Frog** *Hyla meridionalis* 5cm. Small, bright green back, large suckers on finger tips. Not in Britain.

CLUES AND HINTS

When to look: Reptiles and amphibians are found more easily during the summer when they are active. In winter, they hide under stones or in crevices, often appearing dead.

Where to look: In spring, amphibians breed in large numbers in ponds. Remember to watch quietly.

◀ **Green Lizard** *Lacerta viridis* Up to 13cm. Long-tailed lizard. Green back, light-yellow underparts. Lives in southern Europe.

Lizards and Snakes

▶ **Sand Lizard** *Lacerta agilis*
Body 9cm, tail 9cm. Male is green
on sides, especially in spring,
female brown or grey. Both
spotted. Young hatch from eggs
early summer. Coastal sand dunes,
heaths.

◀ **Common Lizard** *Lacerta
vivipara* Body 6.5cm, tail 7cm.
Brown or grey back, white,
orange, yellow or reddish below.
Young born alive, not hatching
from eggs. Grassy and heathy
places.

▶ **Slow-worm** *Anguis fragilis*
50cm. Snake-like, but really a
lizard without legs. Very smooth.
Young golden with dark back
stripe and belly. Eats slugs and
other small animals. Grassy places.

◀ **Grass Snake** *Natrix natrix*
120cm. Eye has round pupil. Grey,
green or brown, black spots or
markings down sides. Usually has
yellow collar. Young hatch from
eggs. Grassy places.

▶ **Adder** *Vipera berus* 65cm.
Head triangular, eye with
slit-like pupil. Grey or brown,
usually with zig-zag. Young
born alive, not from eggs.
Only poisonous snake in
Britain. Many habitats.

◀ **Smooth Snake** *Coronella
austriaca* 60cm. Small head, eyes
with round pupil. Often a dark line
from snout to eye. Young born
alive (not hatched from eggs) in
late summer. Eats mainly lizards.
Sandy heathland. Few areas in
southern Britain.

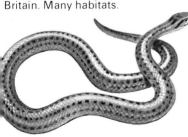

Frogs and Newts

▶ **Common Frog** *Rana temporaria* 10cm. Skin smooth, moist brown patch round ear drum. Hops on long legs. Colour variable with darker spots.

▼ **Edible Frog** *Rana esculenta* 12cm. Whitish vocal sacs bulge from throat when male croaks. More aquatic than common frog. Small colonies in southern England.

Tadpole

♂

▼ **Natterjack Toad** *Bufo calamita* 8cm. Smaller than common toad, head narrower, eyes closer. Brown, grey or green with bright yellow stripe down back. Mainly in sandy and heathy areas.

◀ **Common Toad** *Bufo bufo* 15cm. Skin dry, warty, rough. Large cheek glands. Colour variable, brown, grey or green. Active at night. Damp places.

♂

▶ **Midwife Toad** *Alytes obstetricans* 5cm. Small toad, short legs. Grey or brown. Male carries eggs in spring, dipping them in water to keep moist until ready to hatch. Hides in holes during day, active at night.

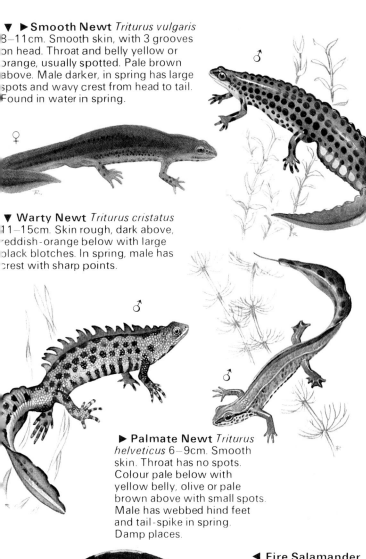

▼ ▶ Smooth Newt *Triturus vulgaris*
8–11cm. Smooth skin, with 3 grooves
on head. Throat and belly yellow or
orange, usually spotted. Pale brown
above. Male darker, in spring has large
spots and wavy crest from head to tail.
Found in water in spring.

♀

♂

▼ Warty Newt *Triturus cristatus*
11–15cm. Skin rough, dark above,
reddish-orange below with large
black blotches. In spring, male has
crest with sharp points.

♂

♂

▶ Palmate Newt *Triturus
helveticus* 6–9cm. Smooth
skin. Throat has no spots.
Colour pale below with
yellow belly, olive or pale
brown above with small spots.
Male has webbed hind feet
and tail-spike in spring.
Damp places.

◀ Fire Salamander
Salamander salamandra
15–28cm. Lizard-like
with short tail.
Distinctive black or
yellow spots and
stripes. Young born
alive. Not in Britain.

Fishes

Fishes are animals with backbones that live in water. They have strong jaws, streamlined bodies covered in scales and fins specialized for swimming. A powerful tail acts as a propeller, and the dorsal and anal fins keep the fish on a straight course. More primitive fishes, like the shark, have skeletons made of cartilage, but most are bony fishes, which have a skeleton made of many bones.

The pectoral and pelvic fins of bony fishes are in pairs and help to stabilize the fish as well as acting as brakes. In most species, a distinct line can be seen down the side of the body – this is known as the lateral line, and it contains sense organs that detect movement in the water. An air bladder inside the body helps to make the fish buoyant, so that it can keep its position in the water without having to go down to the bottom to rest. Bony fishes usually produce many eggs and the male normally sheds 'milt' on them to fertilize them.

The bony fishes are divided into two main groups, the soft-rayed fishes and the spiny-rayed fishes. Soft-rayed fishes have soft fins and include members of the salmon and carp families, the eel, loach, herring, pike, cod and smelt. Spiny-rayed fish, with sharp spines especially on the dorsal fins, include perch, bass, flat fish, gobies, blennies, bullheads, sand eels and scorpion fish.

External Features of a Fish

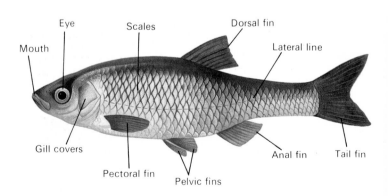

Eye Scales Dorsal fin

Mouth Lateral line

Gill covers Anal fin Tail fin

Pectoral fin Pelvic fins

64

All these fish breathe by passing water over their gills, taking it through the mouth and expelling it through the gill covers. The gills have a rich supply of blood vessels which extract oxygen from the water. Fish vary in the amount of oxygen they need, trout requiring well-oxygenated water to survive, while fish such as the carp need far less oxygen and can live in more stagnant water. Some species can even survive a great range of conditions. Migrating fish, like the salmon and sea trout, start life in fresh water, spending two or three years in the river in which they hatched before descending to the salt sea. They spend the next year or two there, adapting easily to saltwater conditions. When mature, they return again to the freshwater river to spawn. The eel, on the other hand, familiar as a young elver and adult eel in fresh water, returns to the sea to breed.

◀ **River Lamprey**
Lampetra fluviatilis
13–50cm. Belongs to a group of fish-like animals. A sucking mouth enables it to attach itself to the fish on which it feeds.

CLUES AND HINTS

Where to look: You can see freshwater fishes in rivers, canals, ponds, lakes and streams and small marine fishes in shallow water and rock pools on the coast, but they are very difficult to observe closely.

Colour changes: Many males alter their colour during the breeding season. Salmon and sea trout, for example, develop red and pinkish bellies and the grayling's dorsal fin turns red.

What to look for: Some fish are very good at camouflage. A common device is 'counter-shading', where the back is dark, the belly and sides light or silvery. Spots break up the outline of the sea trout and the mackerel has ripple markings, making both hard to see.

How to look: Be very quiet and still when watching fish. Don't let your shadow fall on the water as this can disturb them.

Freshwater Fishes

◀ **Salmon** *Salmo salar* Up to 150cm. Fish from sea, silvery, back darker, few small black spots. Breeding male has hooked jaw. Leaps out of water while travelling up river to lay eggs (spawn).

▶ **Brown Trout** *Salmo trutta* Up to 100cm. Colour brown with lighter belly, spotted red and black. Young trout easily confused with young salmon but pectoral fin orange. Common in fresh water.

◀ **Rainbow Trout** *Salmo gairdneri* Up to 70cm. Colour brown, with reddish irridescent band along sides, heavily spotted all over including tail. Introduced from North America to lakes and ponds in Britain.

▶ **Grayling** *Thymallus thymallus* 50cm. Long striped dorsal fin, turns red on male in breeding season. Swims in shoals in swift streams. Feeds mainly on insect larvae on stream bed.

◀ **Pike** *Esox lucius* 40–100cm. Long duck-like snout sharp backward pointing teeth. Eats mainly other fishes Lakes, ponds and rivers with weed growth.

▶ **Perch** *Perca fluviatilis* Up
to 30cm. Dorsal fin spiny.
Colour greenish-yellow with
dark bands. Often living in
shoals in rivers, lakes and
ponds with weed growth.
Throughout Britain.

◀ **Stone Loach**
*Noemacheilus
barbatulus* Up to 20cm.
4 'whiskers' (barbels)
round mouth. Active at
night in cool, clear lakes
and streams. Feeds on
other small animals.

▶ **Three Spined Stickleback**
Gasterosteus aculeatus Up to
10cm. 3 spines on back with non-
spiny fin behind. Spines on belly.
Ponds and rivers and sometimes
in the sea. The similar Ten spined
stickleback *Pungitius pungitius*
has 7 to 12, although generally 9,
spines on back.

◀ **Eel** *Anguilla anguilla* Up to
100cm. Long, ribbon-like, with
dorsal fin extending to tail and
anal fin similar below. Yellow-
brown in colour until ready to
migrate to the sea to breed, when
it becomes black with silver belly.
It can travel overland.

▶ **Bullhead** *Cottus
gobio* 8–10cm. A spiny
fish with a broad, heavy
head. Hides under
stones in fresh running
water.

Freshwater Fishes

▶ **Roach** *Rutilus rutilus* Up to
30cm. Back dark green, blue or
brown, sides and belly silvery-
white. One of the commonest
fishes in still and slow-moving
waters.

◀ **Carp** *Cyprinus
carpio* Up to 100cm. 4
'whiskers' by mouth.
Body thick, covered in
large scales. Still or
slow-moving water.
Active mainly by night.

▶ **Dace** *Leuciscus leuciscus* Up
to 20cm. Sometimes has golden
sheen on belly. Lower fins pink or
yellowish. Occurs in shoals
in fast-flowing water.

◀ **Tench** *Tinca tinca* Up to
25cm. 2 'whiskers' by mouth.
Eyes small, red. Skin slimy,
olive to black in colour.
Golden ornamental variety.
Weedy and muddy ponds and
slow-moving rivers.

▼ **Silver Bream** *Blicca bjoerkna*
Up to 30cm. Body flattened
sideways. Long anal fin. Small
head, tail deeply forked. Colour
silvery with greenish back
Deep water.

▲ **Common Bream**
Abramis brama 30—50cm.
Deep body, flattened
sideways. Young bream
silvery. Quiet deep waters,
often in shoals.

► **Rudd** *Scardinius erythrophthalmus* 20–30cm. In warm, shallow waters with plenty of weeds. Feeds on plants and animals.

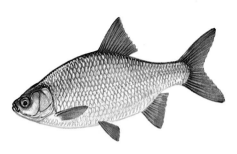

◄ **Chub** *Squalius leuciscus* Up to 20cm. Mouth large. Male has white spots on head in spring. Common in running water, often in large shoals. Eats all kinds of water creatures and leaps out at flying insects.

► **Minnow** *Phoxinus phoxinus* Up to 10cm. Brown or green on back with yellow stripe down side. Silver below, but male has red belly in spring. Cool, clean water with sand or gravel bottom. In shoals.

◄ **Gudgeon** *Gobio gobio* Up to 15cm. 2 'whiskers' by mouth. Blotches on sides. Lives on bottom of sandy or gravelly fast-flowing rivers. Occasionally in lakes. Eats other animals.

► **Barbel** *Barbus barbus* Up to 50cm. 4 large 'whiskers' by mouth. Thick lips. Belly flattened beneath. Lives in shoals near bottom of fast-flowing rivers.

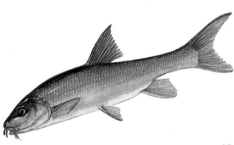

69

Coastal Fishes

▶ **Cod** *Gadus morhua* Up to
100cm. 3 dorsal, 2 anal fins.
'Whisker' on lower jaw. Greenish-
yellow or brown. Cold waters.

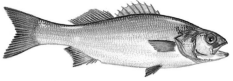

◀ **Bass** *Dicentrarchus
labrax* Up to 80cm. 2
dorsal fins, front one
spiny. Spines on gill
covers. Coastal waters.

▶ **Whiting** *Merlangius
merlangus* Up to 50cm. 3 dorsal,
2 anal fins. Dark spot at base of
pectoral fin. Dark grey or blue
back. Coastal waters, especially
over muddy bottoms.

◀ **Dab** *Limanda limanda* Up
to 40cm. Dorsal and anal fins
along length of body which is
flattened, right side
uppermost. Dark brown,
yellowish or grey below. Lies
flat on sand in coastal waters

▶ **Flounder** *Platichthys flesus*
Up to 50cm. Fins as dab along
length of body, right side
uppermost. Rows of rough warts
on lateral line and base of fins.
Olive-brown or brown above.
Sandy coasts and estuaries.

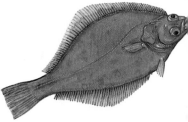

◀ **Plaice** *Pleuronectes
platessa* Up to 60cm. Dorsal
and anal fins along length of
body. Flattened body has
right side uppermost. Brown
with red spots. Sandy coasts
and estuaries, often in deep
water.

► Common Goby

Pomatoschistus microps Up to 11 cm. Short blunt head, large eyes close together. Very well camouflaged in sandy pools in which it lives.

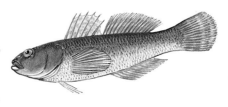

◄ Sand Smelt *Atherina presbyter*

Up to 20cm. Small silvery fish with olive-green back and silvery-white stripe along sides. Scales outlined with black points. Lives in shoals on sandy bottoms in calm bays and estuaries.

► Montagu's Blenny

Blennius montagui Up to 10cm. Round head with two tentacles and flap of skin above eyes. Long dorsal fin dipping in middle. Mottled appearance gives camouflage in rock pools.

◄ Scorpion Fish *Taurulus bubalis*

Up to 15cm. Large head, flattened body. Large pectoral fins, 5 spines on gill covers. Brown blotches on paler background match the seaweed in which it lives. Common in shore pools.

► Greater Sand Eel

Ammodytes lanceolatus Up to 30cm. Eel-like body, greenish above, pale below, with silvery line on sides. Dorsal fin continuous along back. Lower jaw long, used for burrowing in sand when disturbed. Often in shoals over sandy bottoms.

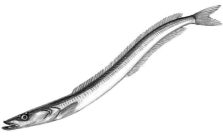

Insects and other Invertebrates

The largest group in the animal kingdom is the invertebrates —
animals without backbones. This group includes the insects, with
their hard outer skeleton, a segmented body and jointed limbs. Most
of them can fly. The body is divided into three distinct parts: the
head, thorax and abdomen. The thorax has three pairs of legs
attached to it, and usually two pairs of wings — except the true flies,
which have only one pair, and others which have none at all. Some
insects have both pairs of wings the same size, others have larger
forewings than hindwings. The front wings of beetles are very tough
and form a protective shield for the body.

The life history of insects varies considerably, but there are two
main types. In one form, the young resemble small adults (nymphs),
and shed their skins and grow until the adult winged stage is reached.
The other form has completely different adult and young types. An
example is the butterfly, which changes from a caterpillar (larva) to
a pupa, then into the adult winged insect. Insects are classified in
different orders according to their life histories and structure,
especially the mouth parts. They are so numerous that only a selec-
tion of species has been illustrated in the following pages.

External Features of an insect
(side view)

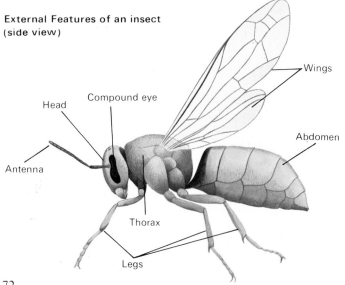

Wings

Compound eye

Head

Abdomen

Antenna

Thorax

Legs

▲ **Silver Y Moth** *Plusia gamma*
4cm. Brown-coloured moth, white
Y mark on forewings. Visitor to
Britain.

▲ **Praying Mantis** *Mantis
religiosa* Up to 7cm. Green, front
legs adapted for catching prey.
Not in Britain.

The kind of food an insect eats affects the shape of its mouth parts.
Moths and butterflies, for example, have a long tongue (proboscis)
used for sucking nectar, while locusts have cutting mouth parts for
gnawing at leaves. Yet insects are constantly in danger of being
eaten themselves by other animals. Some protect themselves by
camouflage, like the patterned wings of certain moths which make
them impossible to see against the bark of trees, some are brightly
coloured to warn off predators and some sting, bite or release
poison. Shape can be a camouflage too: there are insects which look
like twigs, leaves, grass and even seeds.

CLUES AND HINTS

Where to look: Insects are
everywhere, on earth and in
water, on grass and flowers,
on leaves and tree bark, even
in houses. Look carefully at
old trees, hedges and on
ponds, where you will find
more species than in gardens.
When to look: There are
more insects about in the
summer months, but they can
be found all year round.

How to look: Insects are
small and often move very
fast, so they are difficult to
observe. Choose a small patch
of territory and learn to look
closely for a long time. The
insect may be hiding under a
leaf or flat against a twig,
protecting itself from predators. Jot down all the details
you can and do an accurate
drawing.

Butterflies

All measurements are across a single forewing

▶ **Swallowtail** *Papilio machaon* 32–38mm. Large butterfly with black and yellow pattern. Flight strong and quick. Spring, late summer. Caterpillar green with black rings, yellow spots, feeding on milk parsley.

▶ **Small White** *Pieris rapae* 20–26mm. Similar to large white, smaller size. Male 1 to 2 black spots, female 3. Hindwing underside is yellow when closed. Caterpillar green with yellow stripe. Common everywhere in summer.

◀ **Large White** *Pieris brassicae* 29–34mm. Similar to small white. Female 2 black spots on forewing. Male without.

▶ **Orange Tip** *Anthocharis cardamines* 21–25mm. Male distinctive orange patch on tip of forewing; hindwing patchy grey. Female similar with no orange patch; hindwing strongly mottled when wings folded. Caterpillar green. Common woods and hedgerows.

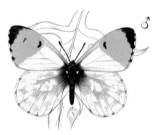

◀ **Clouded Yellow** *Colias crocea* 23–27mm. Yellow-black border. Summer migrant.

▶ **Brimstone** *Gonepteryx rhamni* 26–30mm. Male brilliant yellow with red spots. Female yellowish-green. Green caterpillar. Woodland.

► **Peacock** *Inachis io* 27– 35mm. Attractive butterfly with 'peacock' eyes on wings. Female slightly larger. Underside dark brown. Flight strong, direct. Caterpillar black, feeds on nettles. Common.

♂

◄ **Purple Emperor** *Apatura iris* 31–37mm. Large dark butterfly, usually flies in tree tops. Female larger and without purple. Caterpillar green with yellow stripes. Deciduous woodland.

► **White Admiral** *Limenitis camilla* 26–30mm. Undersides yellowish-brown. Caterpillar yellowish-green. Feeds on honeysuckle. Deciduous woodlands.

◄ **Red Admiral** *Vanessa atalanta* 28–31mm. Underside forewing pattern paler; hindwing patches dark and light brown. Black caterpillar, yellow stripe, feeds on nettles.

► **Painted Lady** *Vanessa cardui* 27– 29mm. Female larger. Underside shows pattern but darker. Caterpillar feeds on thistles. Summer migrant.

Butterflies

▶ **Small Tortoiseshell** *Aglais urticae* 22–25mm. Female larger. Underside shows pattern but darker. Black caterpillar feeds on nettles.

◀ **Camberwell Beauty** *Nymphalis antiopa* 30–35mm. Broad yellow, or, in most British specimens, whitish edges to wings. Migrant.

▶ **Comma** *Polygonia c-album* 22–24mm. Easily recognized by jagged edge to wings. Underside dark, with white C on hindwing. Woodland edges.

◀ **Silver-washed Fritillary** *Argynnis paphia* 33–38mm. Underside hindwing greenish with silver stripes. Woodland clearings.

▶ **Heath Fritillary** *Mellicta athalia* 18–20mm. Orange-brown and yellow markings give a chequered appearance. Underside paler, hindwings whitish. Flowery meadows.

◀ **Pearl-bordered Fritillary** *Clossiana euphrosyne* 19–23mm. Similar in size to heath fritillary, spotted not chequered. Underside of hindwing has silver spots. Open grassland and heaths.

▲ Marbled White *Melanargia galathea* 23−26mm. Female larger. Underside paler. Meadows, early summer.

♀

► Small Heath *Coenonympha pamphilus* 14−17mm. Underside hindwing grey or blue-brown with white mark. Common on open grassland.

► Speckled Wood *Pararge aegeria* 19−22mm. Dark brown with large cream spots. Underside similar. Caterpillar feeds on grasses. Open woodland.

▲ Ringlet *Aphantopus hyperantus* 20−24mm. Male dark brown. Female light brown. Underside of both sexes usually has 7 black spots, circled in white. Open grassland.

◄ Meadow Brown *Maniola jurtina* 22−25mm. Male has smaller orange patches, often none at all. Underside hindwing has broad pale band. Grasslands.

◄ Wall Butterfly *Lasiommata megera* 19−25mm. Rich orange-brown. Underside pale and spotted. Caterpillar feeds on grasses. Roadsides and hedgerows.

77

Butterflies

◄ **Purple Hairstreak**
Quercusia quercus 12–14mm. Female less purple. Underside light grey with white lines. Oak woodland.

▶ **Green Hairstreak**
Callophrys rubi 13–15mm. Underside bright green with white lines or spots. Heaths with gorse and broom.

▶ **Common Blue**
Polyommatus icarus 14–18mm. Female brown, tinged with blue, orange border to wings. Underside light grey with black and white spots. Grasslands.

◄ **Brown Argus**
Aricia agestis 12–14mm. Dark brown with orange border. Underside grey-brown, similar to common blue. Grassy slopes.

▲ **Small Blue** *Cupido minimus* 10–12mm. Male brown, bluish tinge to wings. Female brown. Underside greyish. Grassy slopes.

▶ **Small Copper** *Lycaena phlaeas* 12–15mm. Forewings orange-red with dark brown border, small spots. Underside of wings paler than top. Common grassy slopes and heaths. Caterpillar feeds on sorrel.

◄ **Small Skipper**
Thymelicus sylvestris 13–15mm. Thick body. Black mark on forewing of male. Underside darker. Rapid darting flight. Grassland.

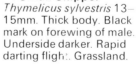

▶ **Grizzled Skipper** *Pyrgus malvae* 11–13mm. Underside pale and blotched. Rapid, darting flight. Caterpillar feeds on strawberries, cinquefoil. Grassland.

Moths

Measurements across forewing.
Male moths have feathery antennae.

▼ **Death's Head Hawkmoth**
Acherontia atropos 45–60mm.
Large, broad body, striped
abdomen. Occasional migrant
from abroad.

▼ **Lime Hawkmoth** *Mimas
tiliae* 30–40mm. Caterpillar
feeds on lime. Common.

▲ **Hummingbird
Hawkmoth** *Macroglossum
stellatarum* 20–30mm. Flies
during the day, hovering like a
hummingbird to suck nectar.

▶ **Buff-tip Moth** *Phalera
bucephala* 21–24mm. At rest,
wings fold like tent. Tufts at base
of wing form hump. Caterpillar
feeds on trees.

Caterpillar

Caterpillar

◀ **Puss Moth** *Cerura vinula* 28–
36mm. Body fluffy. Caterpillar can
puff up front end of body to look
frightening. Feeds on willow,
poplar.

79

Moths

► **Pale Tussock** *Dasychira pudibunda* 21–29mm. Female larger and paler. Caterpillar hairy, feeds on birch, hazel.

▲ **Drinker** *Philudoria potatoria* 30–35mm. Male reddish-brown, female yellower. Caterpillar has tufts of hairs. Damp grassland.

Caterpillar

◄ **Lackey** *Malacosoma neustria* 13–20mm. Small hairy moth. Caterpillars live in large numbers in a tent of silk.

▲ **Lappet** *Gastropacha quercifolia* 27–43mm. Body large, hairy. Looks like a dead leaf at rest. Caterpillar has tufts of hairs.

► **Emperor** *Saturnia pavonia* 28–40mm. Female grey. Male smaller and browner. Flies by day. Caterpillar green with hairy tufts. Feeds on brambles.

▼ **Garden Tiger** *Arctia caja* 37mm. Stout hairy body. Caterpillar hairy, feeds on many plants including nettles. Common.

Caterpillar

► **Cinnabar** *Callimorpha jacobaeae* 18–21mm. Brightly coloured. Caterpillar orange and yellow, common on ragwort.

► **Buff Ermine** *Spilosoma lutea* 20–25mm. Stout hairy body. Caterpillar brown, hairy. Common.

► Yellow Underwing *Noctua pronuba* 26–29mm. Hides underwings when at rest. Caterpillar feeds on grasses, docks, cabbage. Common.

◄ Red Underwing *Catocala nupta* 35–40mm. Forewings cover hindwings at rest, hiding the moth. Caterpillar feeds on poplars. Common.

◄ Large Emerald *Geometra papilionaria* 18–20mm. A number of similar, but smaller, species occur, differing in markings and shape. Caterpillar is a 'looper'

▲ Garden Carpet *Xanthorhoe fluctuata* 12–15mm. Slender body. Caterpillar is a 'looper'.

◄ Magpie *Abraxas grossulariata* 17–21mm. Markings on wings vary but black and white spots with orange patches are distinctive. Caterpillar is a 'looper', feeds on fruit bushes.

Caterpillar

♀

▲ Peppered Moth *Biston betularia* 19–22mm. A black form became widespread in industrial areas when smoke pollution was a problem. Caterpillar is a 'looper' on oak, elm, poplar.

▲ Bordered White *Bupalus piniaria* 19–22mm. Male pale yellow or white. Female wings more orange. Caterpillar feeds on pine needles.

81

Moths

▶ **Six-spot Burnet** *Zygaena filipendulae* 14–18mm. Antennae with clubbed ends. Flies by day. Caterpillar feeds on clovers. Grassland.

▶ **Codlin Moth** *Cydia pomonella* 7–9mm. Small moth with square forewings. Caterpillar often a pest, feeding on apples and pears.

▶ **Green Tortrix** *Tortrix viridana* 9–11 mm. Small moth with square, green forewings. Caterpillars feed on oaks.

▶ **Common Swift Moth** *Hepialus lupulina* 12–15mm. Short antennae. Fast-flying. White marks often absent, especially on female. Caterpillar often a pest, eating roots of plants.

Caterpilla

♀

◀ **Goat Moth** *Cossus cossus* 30–40mm. Female larger. Caterpillar has goat-like smell and feeds inside tree trunks.

◀ **Hornet Clearwing** *Sesia apiformis* 15–20mm. Resembles wasp but is not narrow in middle. Caterpillar feeds on poplar.

▶ **Plume Moth** *Pterophorus pentadactylus* 12–14mm. Narrow wings are divided into feather-like, white plumes. Weak, jerky flight. Caterpillar feeds on bindweed.

Beetles

Measurements = length

◄ Violet Ground Beetle *Carabus violaceus* 8–34mm. Forewings black with violet sheen. Long legs and large jaws.

► Burying Beetle *Necrophorus humator* 18–28mm. Antennae with orange clubbed ends. Buries carrion for larvae to eat.

♀

► Fur Beetle *Attagenus pellio* 45–50mm. Often found in houses. Larvae eat and damage fur and carpets.

► Green Tiger Beetle *Cicindela campestris* 12–15mm. Runs after prey in sunshine and catches it with large jaws. Flies well.

♂

◄ Whirligig Beetle *Gyrinus natator* 5–7mm. Small, freshwater beetle. Whirls round on water surface.

◄ Cockchafer *Melolontha melolontha* 20–30mm. Blundering flight, attracted to light at dusk. Adults eat foliage.

◄ Click Beetle *Corymbites cupreus* 11–16mm. If on its back, makes a loud click as it jumps to right itself. Lives in grassland.

◄ Great Diving Beetle *Dysticus marginalis* 35mm. Carnivorous beetle, living in ponds and rivers. Female has striped wings. Male has suckers on front legs.

▲ Devil's Coach Horse *Ocypus olens* 20–25mm. Forewings very short. When disturbed, curls abdomen over back like a scorpion.

♂

▲ Stag Beetle *Lucanus cervus* Male 60–70mm, female 30–40mm. Mouthparts enlarged in male into horn-like structures. Flies in evening.

Beetles

► Wasp Beetle
Clytus arietis 18–25mm. Wasp-like, but harmless. Scuttles over leaves and tree trunks.

▲ Colorado Beetle
Leptinotarsa decemlineata 6–11mm. A potato pest from America. Larvae are pink and fleshy. Adults and larvae eat potato leaves.

► Nut Weevil
Curculio nucum 6–7mm. Long snout, especially in female. Female bores a hole with snout to lay eggs. Larvae feed inside hazel nuts.

◄ Death Watch Beetle *Xestobium rufovillosum* 5–8mm. Head small, rounded, almost covered by shield on thorax. Male makes clicking sound (April, May) to attract female. Larvae destructive, boring into timbers of old buildings.

▲ Mealworm Beetle
Tenebrio molitor 10–17mm. Forewings have long parallel grooves. Larvae live in flour, a pest in stores and mills.

◄ Cardinal Beetle
Pyrochroa coccinea 20–25mm. A flat beetle with feathery antennae. Often seen on flowers. Larvae are carnivorous.

▲ Furniture Beetle
Anobium punctatum 3–5mm. Eggs laid in cracks furniture, larvae bore hole and feed on wood.

▲ Tortoise Beetle
Cassida viridis 7–10mm. At rest, the broad front wings and head shield are pulled down to completely conceal the body. Feeds on various leaves.

▼ Oil Beetle *Meloe proscarabaeus* Male 10m female 36mm. Short forewings. Exudes oil wh disturbed.

◄ Seven-spot Ladybird *Coccinella 7-punctata* 7–8mm. Hard, red forewings with 7 black spots. Larvae like bluish woodlice. Both adults and larvae feed on aphids.

Bugs

▶ **Pondskater** *Gerris lacustris* 10–13mm. Long, thin legs for walking on surface film of fresh water. 1st pair used for catching prey, 2nd pair for swimming, 3rd pair for steering. Ponds and lakes.

◀ **Water Boatman** *Corixa punctata* 13–16mm. Long, flattened hind legs for swimming under water.

▼ **Hawthorn Shield Bug** *Acanthosoma haemorrhoidale* 10–13mm. Triangular-shaped shield covers bases of forewings. Feeds on hawthorn fruit and leaves.

▶ **Assassin Bug** *Reduvius personatus* 18–23mm. Curved piercing mouthparts for sucking juice from prey. Feeds on other insects. Larva covers itself with scraps of rubbish to hide.

▲ **Southern Cicada** *Cicadetta montana* 16–27mm. Normally rests with wings folded, in trees and shrubs. Very difficult to see, but male makes shrill whistle. Nymphs feed on tree roots.

▶ **Leaf Hopper** *Jassus lanio* 6–8mm. Sucks sap of oak leaves. Leaps well. One of many similar species.

◀ **Frog Hopper** *Philaenus spumarius* 5–6mm. Jumps well. Nymphs develop in a 'cuckoo spit'.

▼ **Rose Aphid Greenfly** *Macrosiphum rusae* 2–3mm. Similar to blackfly, but green. Infests various plants and spreads diseases.

▲ **Greenhouse Whitefly** *Trialeurodes vaporariorum* 1–4mm. Small, white sucking bugs with white waxy wings. Occur on undersides of leaves in greenhouses.

▲ **Blackfly** *Aphis fabae* 2–3mm. Round black bugs with long legs and antennae. Winged or wingless. Females can reproduce without mating. Spreads diseases to various crops.

85

Ants and Bees

▲ **Dark Ant** *Formica fusca* 10–15mm. Head narrow, round at back. Common in gardens especially under paved paths.

▲ **Black Ant** *Lasius niger* 3–5mm. Small ant. Common in gardens.

▲ **Wood Ant** *Formica rufa* 5–11mm. Builds large mounds, especially in pine woods.

▼ **White-tailed Bumblebee** *Bombus lucorum* 20–24mm. Black and yellow stripes with white end. Builds nest underground, often in an old mouse hole.

▶ **Honey Bee** *Apis mellifera* 12–20mm. Single female (queen) in nest. Males have no sting. Most bees are workers.

◀ **Cuckoo Bee** *Nomada lineola* 10–12mm. Small bee, looking like wasp. Lays eggs in nests of mining bees.

▼ **Mining Bee** *Andrena armata* 10–12mm. Male dark, female rich brown. Abdomen flattened. Broad hind legs sweep earth. Digs nest burrow with mouth parts.

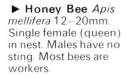

▶ **Leafcutter Bee** *Megachile centuncularis* 9–12mm. Resembles honey bee but darker striped abdomen. Cuts pieces from leaves, especially roses, to build nests.

Wasps

▶ **Common Wasp** *Vespula vulgaris* 11–20mm. One of several very similar species. Builds nest from wood pulp made into 'paper' by chewing. All die in autumn except the new queens which hibernate and start new nests in spring.

◀ **Hornet** *Vespa crabro* 19–35mm. Large wasp. Brown not black markings and deep yellow colour. Papery nests made in hollow trees.

◀ **Potter Wasp** *Eumenes pendunculatus* 15mm. Waist long and narrow. Builds vase-shaped nest from clay, and puts caterpillars in for its young to eat.

▼ **Digger Wasp** *Ammophila sabulosa* 16–28mm. Very long, slender waist. Nests in burrows on sandy soil.

▶ **Horntail** *Urocerus gigas* 10–40mm. No waist. Female larger than male, with black and yellow bands and large egg-laying tube at hind end. Larvae feed on wood.

♂

▶ **Ichneumon Fly** *Rhyssa persuasoria* 30mm. Parasite with very long, slender egg-laying tube. Deposits eggs in wood.

♀

▼ **Hawthorn Sawfly** *Trichiosoma tibiale* 20mm. No waist. Female has egg-laying tube, making slits in plants in which to lay eggs.

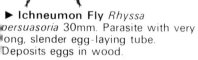

▶ **Gall Wasp** *Biorrhiza pallida* 2–3mm. Grows up inside oak apple – a gall growing on oak trees.

True Flies

► **Bluebottle** *Calliphora vomitoria* 12mm. Large, buzzing fly with shiny metallic blue abdomen.

◄ **Stable Fly** *Stomoxys calcitrans* 5–7mm. Spiky mouth pierces skin of animals, sucks blood.

► **Hover Fly** *Syrphus ribesi* 10–12mm. Usually seen on flowers or hovering with rapidly beating wings, often going backwards. Larvae feed on aphids.

◄ **Bee Fly** *Bombylius major* 8–12mm. A furry, bee-like fly. Sucks nectar with long tongue. Hovers.

▲ **House Fly** *Musca domestica* 7–9mm. Small dark fly; mouthparts mop up liquids. Larvae feed on decaying animal matter.

► **Midge** *Chironomus annularis* 11–15mm. Non-biting midge. Hump behind head. Male has feathery antennae.

▼ **Mosquito** *Culex pipiens* 3–5mm. Male has feathery antennae. Female has pointed mouthparts for sucking blood.

♂

▲ **Robber Fly** *Asilus crabroniformis* 16–30mm. Big eyes and strong, hairy legs help it to catch other insects in flight.

♂

► **Crane Fly** *Tipula maxima* 15–23mm. Male abdomen not pointed. Larvae are pests eating roots of grass.

♀

Other Flies

▼ **Caddis Fly** *Phryganea grandis* 15–21mm. Long, spiky legs. Wings hairy, held like a roof at rest, with antennae pointing forwards. Near water.

▲ **Scorpion Fly** *Panorpa communis* 20mm. Beak-like head. End of male's body turned up like scorpion. Shady places.

▼ **Mayfly** *Isonychia ignota* 15–20mm. 2 long 'tails', hindwings small. Shortlived. Near water.

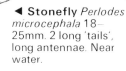

◄ **Stonefly** *Perlodes microcephala* 18–25mm. 2 long 'tails', long antennae. Near water.

▲ **Lacewing** *Chrysopa septempunctata* 30–40mm. Soft green body, wings folded roof-like at rest. Adults and larvae feed on aphids.

◄ **Alder Fly** *Sialis lutaria* 25mm. Wings held roof-like at rest. Found near slow-moving streams. Larvae live in water.

▼ **Snake Fly** *Raphidia notata* 25–29mm. Long neck readily identifies this insect. Female has long egg-laying tube.

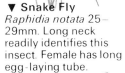

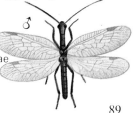

Dragonflies

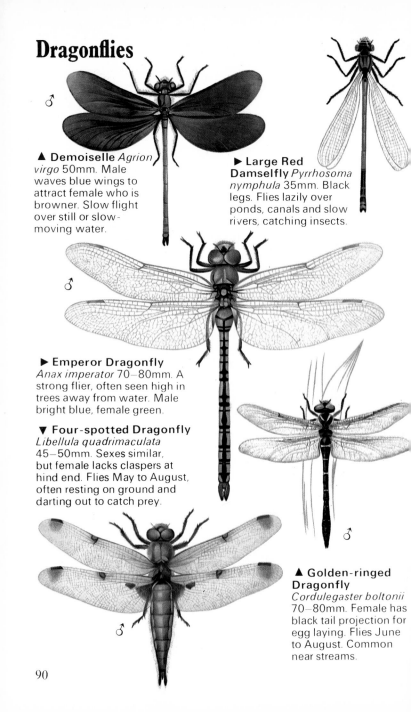

▲ **Demoiselle** *Agrion virgo* 50mm. Male waves blue wings to attract female who is browner. Slow flight over still or slow-moving water.

► **Large Red Damselfly** *Pyrrhosoma nymphula* 35mm. Black legs. Flies lazily over ponds, canals and slow rivers, catching insects.

► **Emperor Dragonfly** *Anax imperator* 70–80mm. A strong flier, often seen high in trees away from water. Male bright blue, female green.

▼ **Four-spotted Dragonfly** *Libellula quadrimaculata* 45–50mm. Sexes similar, but female lacks claspers at hind end. Flies May to August, often resting on ground and darting out to catch prey.

▲ **Golden-ringed Dragonfly** *Cordulegaster boltonii* 70–80mm. Female has black tail projection for egg laying. Flies June to August. Common near streams.

Other Insects

◀ **Meadow Grasshopper**
Chorthippus parallelus 11–24mm.
Forewings leathery, hindwings
minute. Colour variable. Male has
longer front wings and 'sings' by
rubbing legs against wings.

◀ **House Cricket**
Acheta domesticus
16–20mm. Wings of
male rubbed to produce
chirping 'song'. Female
has needle-like egg-
layer. Active at night.

▶ **Field Cricket**
Gryllus campestris 20–
25mm. Male produces
chirping 'song'. Female
has long tube for egg
laying. Lives in burrow.

▶ **Great Green Bush
Cricket** *Tettigonia
viridissima* 28–42mm.
Male rubs wings
against each other to
produce 'song'. Female
has long sword-like
tube for egg laying.

▶ **Common
Cockroach** *Blatta
orientalis* 18–30mm.
Flat, dark brown or
black. Male has longer
wings. Active indoors
at night.

▲ **Earwig** *Forficula
auricularia* 14–23mm.
Front wings very short.
Pincers at end of
abdomen, curved in
male, straighter in
female.

▼ **Cat Flea**
Ctenocephalides felis
5mm. Hard body,
flattened from side to
side. No wings. Sucks
blood. Jumps well with
long hind legs.

▲ **Silver Fish** *Lepisma
saccharina* 7–10mm.
No wings, 3 'tails',
tapering silvery bodies
covered with dust-like
scales.

▲ **Springtail** *Podura
aquatica* 5mm. No
wings. Jumps forward.
Near ponds
and lakes.

▼ **Onion Thrip** *Thrips
tabaci* 1–2mm. Very
small with 2 pairs of
feather-like wings.
Destructive to crops.

▶ **Bark louse** 2mm. One of
many very similar small insects
that live on tree trunks. They
chew pollen grains and algi.

Other Invertebrates

◀ **Garden Spider**
Ataneus diadematus
Male 4—8mm, female
10—15mm. Weaves
circular, sticky webs on
bushes and fences.

▶ **House Spider**
Tegenaria domestica
10—15mm. A fast-
running spider, often
found indoors. Spins
cobwebs in corners.

▼ **Water Spider**
Argyroneta aquatica
10—15mm. Lives under
water in silken tent filled
with air. Reddish-
brown, often looks
silvery due to air trapped
on hairy body.

▲ **Harvestman**
Phalangium opilio 7—
10mm. Not a true
spider. It has only 1
body segment, spiders
have 2.

▲ **Wolf Spider**
Pisaura listera 15—
20mm. Makes no web;
runs after prey to
catch it.

▶ **Harvest Mite**
Trombicula autumnalis
Less than 1mm. 8 legs,
round body, small head.

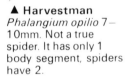

▲ **Centipede**
Lithobius forficatus
25—40mm. Flat body,
with 1 pair of legs to
each segment. Feeds on
other animals.

▶ **Millipede**
Ommatoiulus sabulosus
40—50mm. Body round
rather than flat. 2 pairs
of legs to each segment.
Feeds on plants.

◀ **Earthworm**
Lumbricus terrestris
90—200mm. No head
or legs, but front end is
more pointed. One of
many species.

◄ Medicinal Leech *Hirudo medicinalis* 35–70mm. Worm-like with powerful sucker at hind end. Mouth adapted for sucking blood. Fresh water.

► Woodlouse *Oniscus asellus* 12–15mm. Land-living crustacean, with grey body and 7 pairs of legs. Always in damp places.

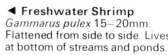

◄ Freshwater Shrimp *Gammarus pulex* 15–20mm. Flattened from side to side. Lives at bottom of streams and ponds.

► Garden Slug *Arion subfuscus* 25–30mm. Long slimy body leaving trail behind. Back is rounded, brown in colour. Long tentacles show when moving.

▲ Great Grey Slug *Limax maximus* 12–15cm. One of the larger slugs. Back keeled, not rounded. Feeds on rotting plants and fungi.

► Great Ram's Horn Snail *Planorbarius corneus* Shell 12–30mm across. Round, brown with 4 to 6 whorls. A pair of tentacles appear when snail moves. Lives in fresh water.

▲ Garden Snail *Helix aspersa* 25–35mm. Shell round with 4 to 5 right-handed whorls. Secretes slimy trail. Eyes at tops of longer tentacles.

◄ Great Pond Snail *Lymnaea stagnalis* 50–60mm. Shell tapers to fine point. One pair of tentacles show when moving. Eyes at base of tentacles. Fresh water.

93

Shells and other Seashore Creatures

Shells are the outer skeletons of soft-bodied animals belonging to a large group of animals called molluscs. The young are often completely different and swim freely before settling down to become adults – either on sandy shores or rocks. Most molluscs can be assigned to two main groups, the univalves (one shell or valve) and the bivalves (two shells or valves). Univalves develop one shell which may be coiled or dome-shaped. They include the snails and limpets. The soft-bodied mollusc fills the shell, and the part emerging from the base of the shell, known as the foot, is used for moving and feeding. Bivalves have two shells, joined together by a hinge, which interlocks and is toothed so that the two halves fit tightly together. Strong muscles keep the shell closed as well as allowing it to open and feed. Small particles of food are sieved from currents of water drawn into the shell.

Bivalve   Single shell (univalve)

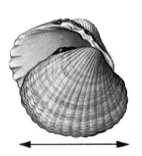
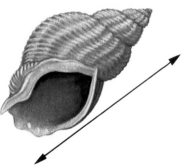

▲ Bivalves are usually measured by width and univalves by length.

Another smaller group of shells, of which the chiton is the most familiar, have a similar internal structure, but the shells are formed into a number of plates, enabling the animal to roll up in case of danger. The last group of molluscs either have very small shells or have lost them altogether. It includes squids and octopuses. Their shells are surrounded by their body. They use long arms with suckers to feed, and have a water-expelling siphon allowing them to swim rapidly when required.

As well as the molluscs, many other creatures can be found on the seashore. One of the largest groups is the crustaceans, which belongs to the same major division of animals as insects. They have a segmented body with a hard outer covering, antennae and legs. This group includes the familiar crab, lobster and shrimp, as well as the barnacle. Sea anemones and jellyfish belong to another group and are quite primitive animals with only a few layers of cells, some of which sting. Jellyfish swim, while anemones are fixed and wait for the sea currents to bring them food. The aquatic worms (ragworm, lugworm), have long segmented bodies, with large heads and numerous bristles. Starfish and sea urchins, on the other hand, are wheel-shaped or globular and walk on special structures called tube feet, which project from their arms. Many of these animals are specialized in the way that they live and only occur on certain parts of the shore.

◀ **Crawfish** *Palinurus vulgaris* 50cm. Like the lobster in shape, but has no large claws on the first pair of legs. Reddish-brown with speckled legs and antennae. Lives in the warm waters of the Mediterranean and Atlantic coasts of Europe to the Channel.

CLUES AND HINTS

Where to look: Sandy shores are good places to look for bivalves, especially at low tide. On rocky shores, many different kinds of shells cling to rocks. Look in crevices and cracks and in pools. Search carefully on muddy shores and estuaries when the tide is out.

How to look: When studying live molluscs, treat them gently and always replace them where you found them. When collecting empty shells on the shore, keep a record of when and where you found them. Clean them and store carefully in cotton wool in labelled boxes.

Single Shells

▶ **Necklace Shell** *Natica alderi* 1.5–3cm long. Rounded, smooth shell with short spiral coil. Common on sand below tide line.

▲ **Whelk** *Buccinum undatum* Up to 12cm long. 6 to 8 whorls separated by deep grooves. Common on muddy, rocky shores.

◀ **Sting Winkle** *Ocenebra erinacea* 6cm long. Pointed spiral shell. 4 to 7 whorls with rough, spiny projections. Common on firm bottoms, jetties, piers.

◀ **Pelican's Foot** *Aporrhais pes-pelecani* 5cm long. Thick shell with 10 to 12 whorls and with long pointed projections at base. Colour variable. Lives below tide line.

▲ **Painted Topshell** *Calliostoma zizyphinum* 4cm high. Pointed with close whorls. Reddish-yellow with red spots. Just below tide line.

▶ **Chinaman's Hat** *Calyptraea chinensis* 7mm high. Low shell, flattened whorls. Attached to rocks, piers, jetties.

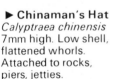

◀ **Keyhole Limpet** *Fissurella costaria* 6cm wide. Flattened, low conical shell with prominent ribs radiating from the keyhole-shaped centre. Yellow-grey. Stony bottoms and rocks.

▶ **Slipper Limpet** *Crepidula fornicata* Up to 5cm wide. White plate inside extending across half the opening. Pest on oyster beds.

▲ **Common Limpet** *Patella vulgata* Up to 6cm wide. Greenish-white or brown with broad dark rays. Clings to rocks between tide lines on rocky coasts. Feeds and moves at night.

◄ **European Cowrie** *Trivia monacha* 4cm long. Small, finely-ribbed shell. White or pink. Rocky shores.

► **Needle Shell** *Bittium reticulatum* 1.2cm long. Whorls have raised bumps forming spiral lines. Common in seaweed. Rocky and muddy shores.

◄ **Wentletrap** *Clathrus clathrus* 3cm long. 12 to 15 whorls with deep grooves between them crossed by thick ridges. Sandy, muddy shores.

► **Tower Shell** *Turritella communis* 5cm long. Spiral lines follow the twist of the shell. Common muddy and sandy shores below low tide line.

▲ **Common Periwinkle** *Littorina littorea* 2–3cm long. Usually slate-coloured with darker spiral bands following the twist of the shell. Common on seaweed between tide lines.

◄ **Flat Periwinkle** *Littorina littoralis* 1.5cm. Shell rounded with flattened top. Few whorls. Colour variable. Occurs on shores where the seaweed bladderwrack grows.

► **Ormer** *Haliotis tuberculata* 6–8cm long. Flat, ear-shaped shell with line of holes near outer edge. Upper whorls tightly coiled. Brown, mother-of-pearl lining. Rocky shores.

▲ **Chiton** *Lepidochitona cinereus* 2–4cm long. 8 overlapping plates enable animal to curl up. Colour variable. Common on or under stones near high tide line.

97

Bivalves

▶ **Oyster** *Ostrea edulis* Up to 15cm wide. Shell thick, brown, chalky. Shape irregular with heavy ridges. Cements itself to stony bottoms in shallow water, especially estuaries.

▶ **Saddle Oyster** *Anomia ephippium* Up to 6cm wide. Smaller than oyster. Orange-brown with white marks. Stony shore near low tide line.

▲ **Queen Scallop** *Chlamys opercularis* Up to 9cm wide. Shape almost circular, with flat hinge. 18–22 prominent ribs. Sandy shores, below low tide line.

◀ **Nut Shell** *Nucula nucleus* Up to 1.2cm wide. Small, thin, flat shell. Common offshore burrowing in sand, mud or silt.

▶ **Cockle** *Cardium edule* 5cm wide. Harvested for food. Common sandy and muddy shores, estuaries.

▲ **Dog Cockle** *Glycymeris glycymeris* 6–10cm wide. Almost circular, thick shell with grooved inner margins and humped hinge. Sandy shores.

◀ **Rayed Artemis** *Dosinia exoleta* Up to 5cm wide. Thick valves, pointed hinge. Common sandy and muddy shores, below low tide line.

▲ **Mussel** *Mytilus edulis* 8cm wide. Blue-grey. White inside with blue edge, shiny. Common, anchored to rocks, jetties, piers.

▲ **Common Otter** *Lutraria lutraria* 13cm wide. Oblong valves, gaping open slightly at each end. Burrows in sand and mud. Common.

◀ **Rayed Trough Shell** *Mactra corallina* 6cm wide. Smooth, thin, triangular or oval. Hinge blunt. Common on sandy shores.

▶ **Piddock** *Pholas dactylus* 15cm wide. Valves long, finger-like at one end. Sharp teeth on edge. Bores holes in wood, soft rocks. Common.

◀ **Baltic Tellin** *Tellina balthica* 2cm wide. Thin, rounded shell. Pointed hinge. Common on muddy shores.

▶ **Blunt Tellin** *Tellina crassa* 5cm wide. Shell thick, rounded. Sandy shores below low tide mark.

▲ **Sand Gaper** *Mya arenaria* 12cm wide. Left valve smaller, valves do not close completely. Burrows in mud and sand. Common.

▲ **Thin Tellin** *Tellina tenuis* 2.5cm wide. Thin, oval valves, remaining together after the animal dies. Sandy shores near low tide mark.

◀ **Banded Wedge** *Donax vittatus* 3cm wide. Oblong shape, shiny surface. Yellow to brown outside, purple, white or yellow inside. Sandy shores near low tide mark.

◀ **Large Razor Shell** *Ensis siliqua* 20cm long. Long, narrow, almost straight shell with hinge nearer to one end. Open at both ends. Burrows, living in holes on sandy shores. Common.

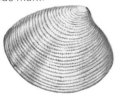

▲ **Striped Venus** *Venus striatula* 3.5cm wide. Valves nearly triangular in shape, with close concentric ridges. Burrows on sandy shores. Common.

▲ **Small Razor Shell** *Ensis ensis* Up to 16cm long. Similar to large razor shell but smaller and more strongly curved. Burrows and lives in holes in sand. Common.

Other Seashore Creatures

▶ **Shrimp** *Crangon vulgaris*
6cm long. Hard segmented body.
5 pairs of walking legs, swimming
'legs' on abdomen. Long antennae.
Burrows in sand. Common.

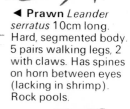

◀ **Prawn** *Leander
serratus* 10cm long.
Hard, segmented body.
5 pairs walking legs, 2
with claws. Has spines
on horn between eyes
(lacking in shrimp).
Rock pools.

◀ **Acorn Barnacle**
Balanus balanoides Up
to 2cm wide. Body
concealed by 6 fused
plates. Legs protrude to
feed. Rocky shores.

▶ **Sea Slater** *Ligia
oceanica* Up to 3cm
long. Hard, segmented
oval, flattened body.
Active at night on high
tide line.

▶ **Sand Hopper**
Orchestia gammarella
Up to 2cm long. Red to
greenish-brown,
flattened sides. Under
stones or seaweed near
high tide line.

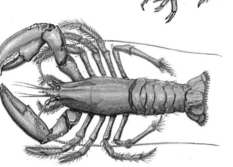

◀ **Lobster** *Homarus
vulgaris* 20–50cm long.
Stout, hard, segmented
body. Large pincers on
one pair of legs. Does
not swim but darts
backwards, using tail
and abdomen. Lives on
rocky coasts below tide
line.

► **Dahlia Anemone**
Tealia felina 5cm wide.
Tentacles thick, red or
pink, white bars. 'Body'
greyish-green,
patterned with red.
Rocky pools.

◄ **Beadlet Anemone**
Actinia equina 3cm
wide. Slender tentacles
with spots at base.
'Body' contracts to
conserve water when
tide is out. Rock pools.

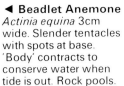

◄ **Starfish** *Asterias
rubens* Up to 40cm
wide. 5 pointed arms.
Mouth central, below.
Lives below tide line.
Common.

▲ **Common Jellyfish**
Aurelia aurita 30–40cm
wide. 4 long arms hang
from mouth. Common.

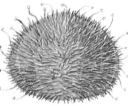

▲ **Sea Urchin** *Echinus
esculentus* 12cm wide.
Colour purple or red.
Sandy shores near low
tide mark.

► **Ragworm** *Nereis
diversicolor* Up to 10cm
long. Lives in burrows,
muddy shores.

► **Lugworm** *Arenicola
marina* 10–25cm long.
Front end thick, tail
thinner. Sandy shores
in 'U' shaped burrows.

◄ **Hermit Crab**
Eupagurus bernhardus
8–10cm long. Soft-
bodied. Lives in other
shells, moving house as
it grows. Common.

► **Shore Crab**
Carcinus maenas 5cm
long. 5 pairs of legs,
front pair with large
pincers. Walks
sideways. Common.

▲ **Cuttlefish** *Sepia
officinalis* Up to 50cm
long. Flat body with fin
around edge. Skeleton
(cuttle bones) often
found on shore.

101

Trees

Trees are plants which have become supremely successful in reaching up to the light and dominating all other forms of plant life. Light is essential to all green plants, as they need it to help in the manufacture of food. The tall trunk of a tree carries its leaves, where the food is manufactured, up into the light and the branches spread the leaves out to catch as much light as possible. Thus trees are the tallest living things, and in Britain some exceed 52 metres. The tallest tree in the world is the coast redwood of California, one of which reaches 113 metres.

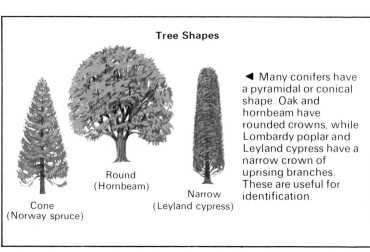

Tree Shapes

◀ Many conifers have a pyramidal or conical shape. Oak and hornbeam have rounded crowns, while Lombardy poplar and Leyland cypress have a narrow crown of uprising branches. These are useful for identification.

Round
(Hornbeam)

Narrow
(Leyland cypress)

Cone
(Norway spruce)

There are two quite distinct groups of trees: conifers with simple flowers bearing their seeds in cones, and broadleaved trees with a variety of more complex flower types. Conifers have simple needle-like or scale-like leaves which are thick and often waxy to avoid water loss. Most are evergreen and keep their leaves for several years. Broadleaved trees have larger, flatter leaves arranged carefully to catch the light. Most are thin and able to absorb and give off gases and water vapour easily whilst manufacturing food (photosynthesis), but cannot stand the rigorous conditions of winter. In northern Europe, many of them are deciduous, that is they drop their leaves in autumn. Broadleaved trees are sometimes called hardwoods because coniferous timber is more easily worked.

Simple unlobed

Hornbeam   Beech

Simple lobed

Common oak   Sycamore

Compound

Horse chestnut   Common ash

Leaf Shapes

Leaf shapes are very varied and the most useful characteristic for identification. Leaves of conifers are narrow, often sharp-pointed. They are very long and held in groups in pines. Scale-like leaves occur on cypresses and several other trees. Most other conifers have numerous needle-shaped leaves. Broadleaved trees have much more varied leaf shapes. Many have simple unlobed oval leaves. Some simple leaves are lobed regularly on each side like the oak, while many leaves have 3 to 5 radiating lobes like the maples. Compound leaves, divided into leaflets, fall into two groups: 'palmate' (hand-shaped) with about 5 lobes radiating from the tip of the leaf stalk and 'pinnate' with leaflets down either side of the stalk.

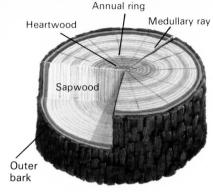

Heartwood
Annual ring
Medullary ray
Sapwood
Outer bark

▲ Section through tree trunk
The bark cracks as a new layer of wood is added each year. The cracks and fissures form distinctive patterns (see below).

The Tree Trunk

When a tree is felled, the structure of the stem can be seen and its age calculated. There are 'annual rings' of wood which have been added under the bark each year, made up of light-coloured spring wood and darker summer wood. This woody material gives the stem great strength. The outer rings conduct water up the tree. The wood in the centre, the 'heartwood', no longer carries water and is darker, but the annual rings can still be seen.

Different Types of Bark

Top row – deciduous   Bottom row – evergreen

English elm

London plane

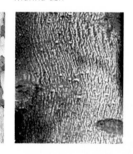

Manna ash

Weymouth pine

Yew

Western hemlock

104

CONIFERS
Larches

◀ **Japanese Larch** *Larix kaempferi*
35m. Blue-green deciduous needles in
rosettes and singly. Twigs orange.
Female flowers cream or greenish.
Round cones with out-turned scales.
Branches horizontal and heavier than
in European larch.

Cone

ng
e

▶ **European Larch**
Larix decidua 38m. Pale
green, soft, deciduous
needles in rosettes and
singly. Female flowers
loganberry-red. Cone
egg-shaped with close
scales.

Cone

105

Cedars and Firs

Cone

▲ **Atlas Cedar** *Cedrus atlantica* 25m.
Needles dark green, or, in garden
forms, blue; in rosettes and singly.
Young trees have ascending branches.
Flowers in autumn and cones take two
years to ripen.

▼ **European Silver Fir**
Abies alba 40m. Flat, dark
green needles spread out to
either side of the shoot.
Narrow crown with short,
level branches and, in old
age, a flat top. Tall, upright
cones, with bracts showing,
break up on tree releasing
seed in first autumn leaving
central spike.

Cone

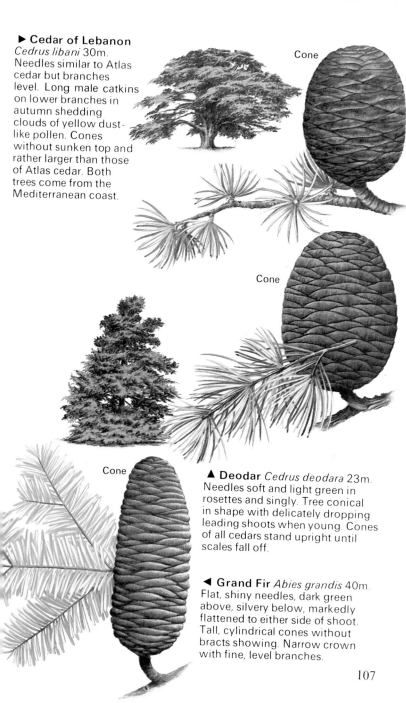

► Cedar of Lebanon

Cedrus libani 30m. Needles similar to Atlas cedar but branches level. Long male catkins on lower branches in autumn shedding clouds of yellow dust-like pollen. Cones without sunken top and rather larger than those of Atlas cedar. Both trees come from the Mediterranean coast.

Cone

Cone

Cone

▲ Deodar *Cedrus deodara* 23m. Needles soft and light green in rosettes and singly. Tree conical in shape with delicately dropping leading shoots when young. Cones of all cedars stand upright until scales fall off.

◄ Grand Fir *Abies grandis* 40m. Flat, shiny needles, dark green above, silvery below, markedly flattened to either side of shoot. Tall, cylindrical cones without bracts showing. Narrow crown with fine, level branches.

107

Firs

◄ Western Hemlock
Tsuga heterophylla
35m. Small, scattered,
flat needles of varying
lengths, dark green
above, two white bands
below. Small hanging
cones with rounded
scales turn from green
to brown and shake out
small black seeds. A
spire-like tree with a
broad base tapering to a
delicately drooping
leading shoot. Branch
ends also droop. A tree
from north western
America well suited to
Britain and growing to a
large size. It will
withstand dense shade
and grows well under
other trees.

Cone

♀ flowers

♂ flowers

Cone

◄ Douglas Fir
Pseudotsuga menziesii
40m. Needles flat and
soft, green above,
whitish below, parted
to show shoot above
and below. Bark
smooth with resin
blisters when young,
becoming corky. Buds
pointed, shiny brown,
like those of beech.
From north western
America and now the
tallest tree in Britain.

Spruces

Flowers with pollen

Cone

▲ **Norway Spruce** *Picea abies*
30m. Small sharp needles on pegs
which remain when they fall. Long,
cigar-shaped hanging cones with
rounded scales. A triangular tree
with regular branching, familiar as
the Christmas tree. Bark orange-
brown. Grows well in moist areas.

▼ **Sitka Spruce** *Picea sitchensis*
35m. Very sharp blue-green
needles on pegs. Bark flakes off.
Light brown hanging cones with
papery scales.

Cone

Pines

Needle cluster   Cone

▲ **Arolla or Swiss Stone Pine**
Pinus cembra 20m. Needles in
fives, stiff, giving foliage a dense
appearance. Crown of tree narrow
due to short, horizontal branches.
Small pointed buds. Egg-shaped
cones with thick cone scales and
fat, edible seeds that take $2\frac{1}{2}$ years
to ripen. The seeds are not shaken
out of the cone as in other pines
but the whole cone is shed when
the seeds are ripe.

▶ **Monterey Pine** *Pinus radiata*
30m. Needles in threes, grass-
green, soft. Has a broad crown
when old. Buds blunt pointed,
fairly large, sticky. Cones squat
with lop-sided base pressed hard
against them, usually in clusters of
three to five. Seed ripens in third
year but cones remain on tree
many years. Comes from a small
area on Californian coast and so
resistant to salt-laden winds.

Cone

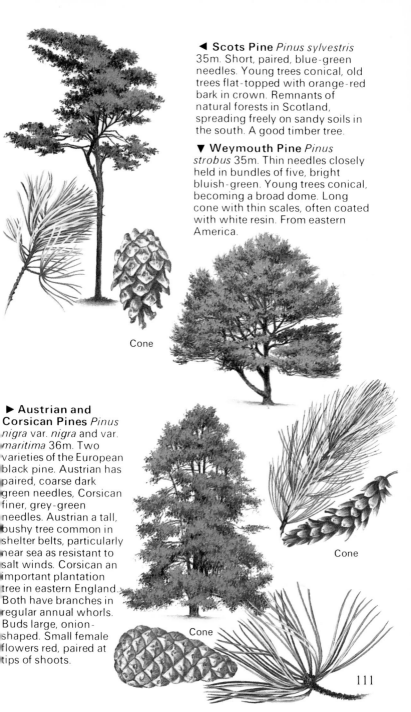

◀ **Scots Pine** *Pinus sylvestris*
35m. Short, paired, blue-green
needles. Young trees conical, old
trees flat-topped with orange-red
bark in crown. Remnants of
natural forests in Scotland,
spreading freely on sandy soils in
the south. A good timber tree.

▼ **Weymouth Pine** *Pinus
strobus* 35m. Thin needles closely
held in bundles of five, bright
bluish-green. Young trees conical,
becoming a broad dome. Long
cone with thin scales, often coated
with white resin. From eastern
America.

Cone

▶ **Austrian and
Corsican Pines** *Pinus
nigra* var. *nigra* and var.
maritima 36m. Two
varieties of the European
black pine. Austrian has
paired, coarse dark
green needles, Corsican
finer, grey-green
needles. Austrian a tall,
bushy tree common in
shelter belts, particularly
near sea as resistant to
salt winds. Corsican an
important plantation
tree in eastern England.
Both have branches in
regular annual whorls.
Buds large, onion-
shaped. Small female
flowers red, paired at
tips of shoots.

Cone

Cone

111

Redwoods

▶ **Giant Sequoia or Wellingtonia**
Sequoiadendron giganteum 38m. Small, sharp, awl-like leaves curve away from twig, similar larger leaves cover twig, both dark green. Light brown bark is thick, soft and fibrous. Tall, regular, spire-like tree, often with lightning-struck top. The descending branches sweep up at ends. A majestic avenue tree from north western America.

Cone

Autumn leaves

Cone

◀ **Dawn Redwood**
Metasequoia glyptostroboides 20m to date. Soft, flat, light green leaves, very similar to swamp cypress but leaves and branchlets oppositely arranged, dropped in winter. Buds arise below branchlets. Young trees pyramidal and regular in outline. Bark fibrous, orange-brown. Stalked green cones rare. Strikes easily from cuttings. Known as a fossil but discovered growing in China in 1941 and introduced widely since.

► Japanese Red Cedar
Cryptomeria japonica 35m. Leaves
awl-like, arranged all round shoot and
curved away from it. Cones round,
spiny, often with shoot growing from
tip.

Cone

Cone

▲ Coast Redwood *Sequoia
sempervirens* 33m. Leaves flat,
dark green above, pale below,
sharp pointed, spread either side
of shoot. Tall, pyramidal with
downswept branches. Thick,
spongy bark. Comes from
California where it is the tallest
tree in the world.

► Swamp Cypress *Taxodium
distichum* 20m. Soft, light green,
feathery leaves, flattened to either
side of shoot. On branchlets
arranged alternately and dropped
in winter. Very regular shaped,
triangular tree with stringy, deeply
furrowed bark.

113

Cypresses

▶ **Lawson Cypress**
Chamaecyparis lawsoniana
25m. Leaves small, evergreen,
scale-like, in fours, one pair
larger than the other, with
white markings below.
Column-shaped, with dense
fine branches to ground. Stem
forked. Many small red male
flowers on shoot-tips in
spring. Small brown cones
with hobnail-like scales.

Cone

Unripe cone

◀ **Leyland Cypress**
x *Cupressocyparis leylandii*
30m to date. Leaves
indistinguishable from
Lawson cypress but a dense
foliaged, broader, more
parallel sided crown, reaching
30m in 50 years. Seldom
cones, but strikes easily from
cuttings. Can be clipped hard
and, with its rapid growth, is
ideal for hedges.

▶ **Monterey Cypress**
Cupressus macrocarpa 25m.
Leaves very small, scale-like,
pointing forwards, dark green
with pale margin. Column-
shaped when young with
dense foliage, becoming flat-
topped when old. Cones are
large, globular, purplish-
brown, with pronounced
knob on scales.

Unripe cone

114

▼ Juniper *Juniperus communis*
6m. Leaves needle-like, sharp
pointed, in threes around stem,
blue-green with white bands on
upper surface. Usually a densely
foliaged, spreading bush. Seeds
in purple berry on female trees.

Unripe cone

Cone

▲ Italian Cypress *Cupressus
sempervirens* 15m. Small, scale-
like, dark green leaves without
points, closely pressed to stem
giving a thread-like appearance.
An upright, very narrow tree.
Large, rounded cones like those
of Monterey cypress with lumps
on cone scales.

Cone

▲ ▶ Western Red Cedar *Thuja
plicata* 30m. Scale-like leaves similar
to Lawson cypress, in flat sprays with
white patches on undersides. Conical
with dense foliage and upright leading
shoot. Bark cinnamon red, soft, peeling
in long strips. Root buttresses at base
of trunk. Cones have few thin, leaf-
like scales.

Other Evergreens

▶ **Chile Pine or Monkey Puzzle**
Araucaria araucana
25m. Leaves are large, stiff and thick with sharp points, dark green, growing all round shoot. Branches in distinct annual whorls until old and flat-topped with bare trunk. Bark grey and roughened by persistent leaf bases. Female cones large, golden shiny globes on separate trees. Seeds large and edible.

Cone

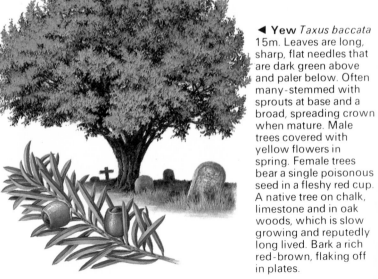

◀ **Yew** *Taxus baccata*
15m. Leaves are long, sharp, flat needles that are dark green above and paler below. Often many-stemmed with sprouts at base and a broad, spreading crown when mature. Male trees covered with yellow flowers in spring. Female trees bear a single poisonous seed in a fleshy red cup. A native tree on chalk, limestone and in oak woods, which is slow growing and reputedly long lived. Bark a rich red-brown, flaking off in plates.

► **Chusan Palm** *Trachycarpus fortunei* 11m. Fan-shaped leaves with long stalks, divided into about 30 long, narrow segments, crowded at top of shaggy stem. Grown only in south and west of Britain.

▼ **European (Dwarf) Fan Palm** *Chamaerops humilis* 4m. Fan-shaped leaves with long stalks and 12–15 segments. Growing naturally in Mediterranean, does not form a stem, but in cultivation produces a fibrous trunk of several metres clothed with old leaf bases. Occasionally grown in southern Britain.

BROADLEAVED TREES
Poplars and Willows

Winter

◄ ►**White Poplar** *Populus alba* 20m. Leaves alternate, lobed, dark green above, white below. Buds white and hairy. Upper bark white with large, diamond-shaped markings. Open, rounded crown.

►**Lombardy Poplar** *Populus nigra* var. *italica* 28m. Leaves alternate, triangular, pointed, with small, regular teeth. Glossy green above with translucent margin, paler below. Narrow crown with close, upright branches and fluted trunk. A natural variation of black poplar.

Summer leaves

♀ catkins

◄ **Aspen** *Populus tremula* 20m. Leaves alternate, round, thin with wavy margin on flattened leaf stalk which causes them to flutter. A small, conical tree with light, open branches. Bark diamond-marked. Occurs in groups.

Autumn leaf

◀ Black Italian Poplar
Populus x *euramericana* var. *serotina* 40m. Leaves alternate, triangular, emerge bronze and turn a light, fresh green. Leaf stalk flattened. A large, open crown with some heavy, upswept branches, stem straight and clear of branches. One of the many hybrids resulting from crosses between European and American black poplars.

Winter

▶ White Willow *Salix alba*
20m. Leaves alternate, long, pointed, with regular teeth, grey-green above, dense white hairs below. Ascending branches form narrow crown. The bark is a network of ridges. Male and female flowers are green catkins on separate trees. One of the common weeping willows, 'Chrysocoma' is a white willow.

♀ catkin

◀ Crack Willow *Salix fragilis* 15m. Leaves alternate, very long and narrow, bright, glossy green above, grey below, not hairy. Broad open crown with hanging branches. Orange twigs snap easily. Grows near water. Branches are often cut back to trunk.

♀ catkins

Willow and Hazel

▶ **Goat Willow** *Salix capraea* 7m. Leaves alternate, oval with a rounded base, a short point at tip and wavy margin. Dark green above, dense grey hairs below, leathery. Leaf stalk also hairy. Large, pointed, bright red buds in winter. A small bushy tree with rounded crown. Twigs thick and knobbly. The true 'pussy willow' – with rounded male flowers covered in grey, silky hairs and yellow pollen when ripe. Female flowers similar, turning green. Common on waste ground and scrub woodland.

♀ catkin

♂ catkins

♀ flowers

♂ catkins

Autumn leaf

Ripe nut

◀ **Hazel** *Corylus avellana* 12m. Leaves alternate, rounded with stiff hairs. Long male catkins (lamb's tails) open yellow from December. Female flowers a tight bud with only two scarlet styles protruding. Nuts in green leafy bracts. Usually a many-stemmed bush; occasionally a small tree. Frequently coppiced. Common.

Alder and Birch

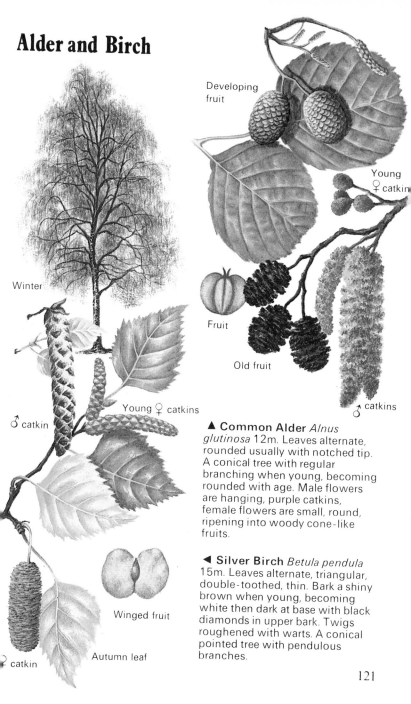

Developing fruit

Young ♀ catkin

Winter

Fruit

Old fruit

♀ catkin

Young ♀ catkins

♂ catkin

♀ catkin

Winged fruit

Autumn leaf

♂ catkins

▲ **Common Alder** *Alnus glutinosa* 12m. Leaves alternate, rounded usually with notched tip. A conical tree with regular branching when young, becoming rounded with age. Male flowers are hanging, purple catkins, female flowers are small, round, ripening into woody cone-like fruits.

◀ **Silver Birch** *Betula pendula* 15m. Leaves alternate, triangular, double-toothed, thin. Bark a shiny brown when young, becoming white then dark at base with black diamonds in upper bark. Twigs roughened with warts. A conical pointed tree with pendulous branches.

121

Hornbeam and Beech

▶ **Hornbeam**
Caprinus betulus 10m.
Leaves alternate, oval,
double-toothed with 15
pairs of pronounced
parallel veins. A small,
bushy tree with a broad
crown and fluted trunk.
Bark silvery-grey, only
occasionally fissured.
Female catkins a leafy
green, appearing with
leaves, ripening to
hanging bunches of
3-pronged bracts
holding brown nutlets.
Only in southern
England. Often
pollarded.

♂ catkin

Fruit

Winter

Winter twig

▼ **Beech** *Fagus sylvatica* 25m.
Leaves alternate, oval with wavy
margin. Light green at first, darkening as
summer proceeds. A tall slender tree
with a few branches in woodlands,
heavy, spreading branches in open
land. Bark smooth, grey, becoming
only slightly fissured in some trees.
Prickly 4-valved fruit contains 2
nutlets.

Autumn

Ripe nut in husk

Winter bud

Chestnut and Oak

▼ **Sweet Chestnut**
Castanea sativa 25m. Leaves alternate, long, toothed with prominent parallel veins. Spreading branches form a massive crown. Flowers mid-summer, fruits spiny.

Summer and autumn leaves

Winter

Nut

Fruit

▼ **Holm Oak** *Quercus ilex* 20m. Alternate evergreen leaves, narrow, dark green above, buff or white below. Young leaves on lower part of tree often sharp-toothed, resembling holly leaves. A rounded, dense crown, often with more than one stem. The small acorn is half enclosed in a fawn-coloured cup with felted scales. Mediterranean tree popular in Britain.

Ripening acorns

123

Oaks

◀ **Sessile Oak** *Quercus petraea* 21m. Leaves alternate, lobed with veins running to the tips of the lobes. Leaves stalked, acorns stalkless and rounded at tip. Crown fan-shaped with upswept branches arising at different levels on the long stem. Occurs naturally on light soils and in upland western Britain.

▶ ▼ **Common Oak** *Quercus robur* 23m. Leaves alternate, rounded lobes with veins to lobes and to indentations. 'Ears' at base of leaf either side of very short leaf stalk. Acorns on long stalks, tall and parallel-sided, usually paired. Rounded crown with short bole due to horizontal branches all arising at same level. Occurs on lime-rich loams and clays.

Winter

◀ **Cork Oak** *Quercus suber* 16m. Alternate, evergreen leaves with wavy margins and very shallow, spine-tipped lobes; dark green above, grey below. A low, spreading crown with twisted trunk and branches. Bark grey, thick and corky, deeply fissured. Acorn cup has wavy margin and only loosely holds acorn. From southern Europe, only in parks and gardens in Britain.

▼ **Turkey Oak** *Quercus cerris* 25m. Leaves alternate, dark green and shiny above, hairy below, deeply and regularly lobed with paired stipules at base. Buds whiskered. The tall, narrow acorn which takes two years to ripen is set deeply in a stalkless 'mossy' cup covered with long, pointed scales. A tall, fast-growing tree with uprising branches forming a wide crown.

♀ flower

♂ catkins

Maples and Plane

▼ ► **Norway Maple** *Acer platanoides* 15m. Leaves opposite, fan-shaped with 5 sharply-pointed lobes. Thin, shiny, bright green. Bud scales brown. A medium-sized tree with an open regular crown, less dense than sycamore. Seeds in pairs at a wide angle.

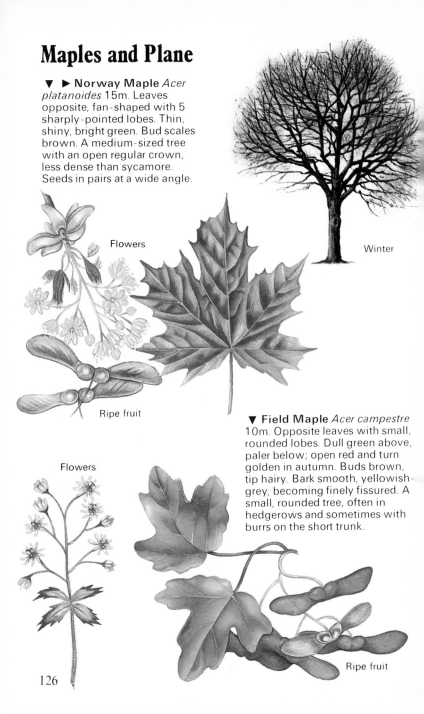

Flowers

Winter

Ripe fruit

Flowers

▼ **Field Maple** *Acer campestre* 10m. Opposite leaves with small, rounded lobes. Dull green above, paler below; open red and turn golden in autumn. Buds brown, tip hairy. Bark smooth, yellowish-grey, becoming finely fissured. A small, rounded tree, often in hedgerows and sometimes with burrs on the short trunk.

Ripe fruit

Flowers

Seed

Winter

▲ **Sycamore** *Acer pseudoplatanus* 20m. Large, opposite leaves with 5-pointed lobes, dark green, leathery. Large green buds. A large tree with a dense, spreading crown. Paired seed wings, closely angled. Seeds freely all over Britain and grows well, even in exposed places.

▶ **London Plane** *Platanus x hispanica* 30m. 5-lobed leaves like a maple but alternate and bright green. Smooth, grey bark flakes off to leave yellow patches. A tall tree with a clean stem and large spreading branches forming a broad crown. Round, spiky bobble-like fruits hang on long stalks all winter. A hybrid between oriental and American plane which arose naturally and has proved ideal for city use, so a common street and park tree.

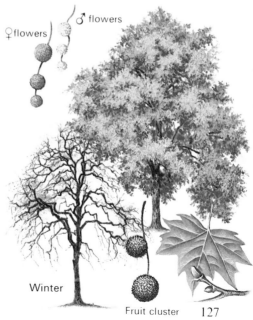

♀ flowers   ♂ flowers

Winter

Fruit cluster

127

Horse Chestnut and Limes

Opening bud

▼ Horse Chestnut *Aesculus hippocastanum* 25m. Opposite, hand-shaped, dark green leaves with 5 to 7 stalkless leaflets, narrow at base and broadening to tip. Large sticky buds. Rich brown seeds (conkers) in spiny green case. Short trunk with few heavy branches upturned at the ends.

Fruit opening to show conker

Seed

Winter

Winter

▲ ▶ Common Lime *Tilia* x *europaea* 25m. Alternate, heart-shaped leaves with tufts of hairs in vein axils below. Buds red-brown with one large and one small scale. Round ribbed fruits hang from leafy wing. Domed crown with arching branches.

▶ Small-leaved Lime *Tilia cordata* 20m. The heart-shaped leaf is nearly round and has orange hairs in vein axils below. Buds lop-sided. A tall domed tree with arching branches. Sprouts and burrs common at base of trunk. Popular avenue tree.

Seed

Elms

Flowers

Ripening Seed

▶ **Wych Elm** *Ulmus glabra*
20m. Leaves alternate, oval,
large, unequal base with one
side covering stalk. Dark
green, rough. Buds large and
hairy. Broad, rounded crown.
Seed in centre of round,
notched wing.

Winter

Seed

Winter twig

Winter

▲ **English Elm** *Ulmus procera* 30m.
Small, alternate leaves with lop-sided
base. Dark green, rough and hairy.
Buds small. A tall domed tree with few
large branches. Suckers freely and
often several hedgerow trees are
connected by common root system.
Common in southern England before
Dutch elm disease.

Flowers

Seed

Ash and Walnut

♂ flowers

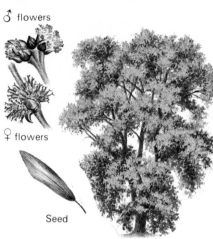

♀ flowers

Seed

◀ **Ash** *Fraxinus excelsior* 25m. Opposite leaves divided into 9 to 13 toothed leaflets on short stalks, terminal leaflet longer-stalked. Comes into leaf late, after the bunches of purplish hanging flowers. Buds large, black, shaped like a bishop's mitre. Bark grey becoming shallowly fissured. A tall tree with sparse ascending branches forming an open crown casting little shade. Single seeds hang in clusters on tree throughout winter.

▶ **Manna Ash** *Fraxinus ornus* 20m. Opposite leaves divided into 5 to 9 leaflets on short stalks, hairs on underside beside veins. Buds brown. Creamy-white flowers borne in dense heads in June when the tree is in full leaf.

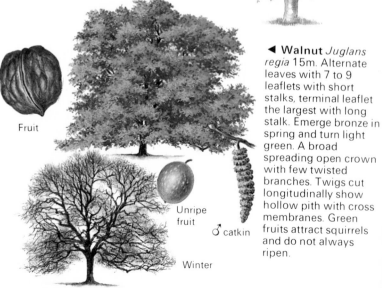

Fruit

Unripe fruit

♂ catkin

Winter

◀ **Walnut** *Juglans regia* 15m. Alternate leaves with 7 to 9 leaflets with short stalks, terminal leaflet the largest with long stalk. Emerge bronze in spring and turn light green. A broad spreading open crown with few twisted branches. Twigs cut longitudinally show hollow pith with cross membranes. Green fruits attract squirrels and do not always ripen.

Rose Family

▶ Hawthorn

Crataegus monogyna
8m. Leaves alternate
with 3 to 7 rounded
lobes, dark green with
leafy stipules at base of
leaf stalk. Twigs have
sharp thorns. Bole
fluted and furrowed. A
small much-branched
tree with rounded
crown. White, scented
flowers in May turn to
dark red haw berries in
autumn which attract
birds.

▼ Rowan *Sorbus*

aucuparia 7m.
Alternate leaves of 9 to
15 stalkless leaflets
with forward-pointing
teeth. Large, hairy, oval
buds. Smooth grey
bark with orange
breathing pores. A
small, slender tree with
few ascending
branches and narrow
crown. In May, cream-
white flowers, in late
summer, red berries
attract birds.

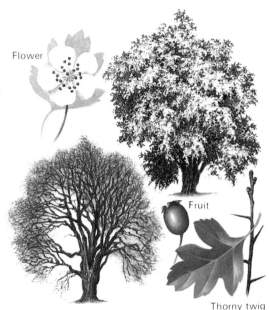
Flower

Fruit

Thorny twig

Winter

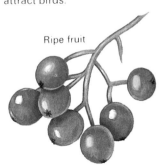
Ripe fruit

Winter

131

Rose Family

Flowers

Ripe fruit

▲ **Whitebeam** *Sorbus aria* 8m.
Alternate oval leaves, double-
toothed; green above, felted with
white hairs below. Bud also hairy.
A small, compact crown formed of
upswept branches on a short stem.
Bark is smooth, pale grey. Creamy-
white sweet-scented flowers in
May. Scarlet berries attract birds.

▼ **Crab Apple** *Malus sylvestris*
10m. Leaves alternate, long to
oval, toothed with white hairs on
undersides. A broad-crowned
tree or shrub, often leaning. Large
pinkish-white flowers. The green
apple only turns partly red when
ripe and is bitter. In hedgerows
and copses.

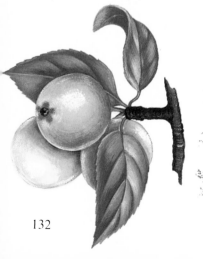

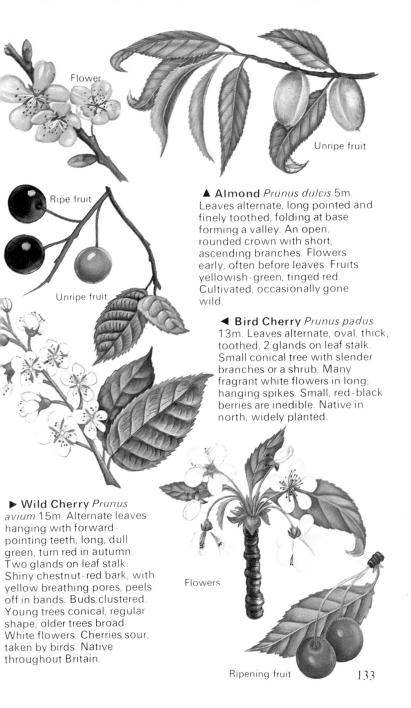

Flower

Unripe fruit

Ripe fruit

Unripe fruit

▲ Almond *Prunus dulcis* 5m.
Leaves alternate, long pointed and finely toothed, folding at base forming a valley. An open, rounded crown with short, ascending branches. Flowers early, often before leaves. Fruits yellowish-green, tinged red. Cultivated, occasionally gone wild.

◄ Bird Cherry *Prunus padus* 13m. Leaves alternate, oval, thick, toothed, 2 glands on leaf stalk. Small conical tree with slender branches or a shrub. Many fragrant white flowers in long, hanging spikes. Small, red-black berries are inedible. Native in north, widely planted.

► Wild Cherry *Prunus avium* 15m. Alternate leaves hanging with forward-pointing teeth, long, dull green, turn red in autumn. Two glands on leaf stalk. Shiny chestnut-red bark, with yellow breathing pores, peels off in bands. Buds clustered. Young trees conical, regular shape, older trees broad. White flowers. Cherries sour, taken by birds. Native throughout Britain.

Flowers

Ripening fruit

133

Pea Family

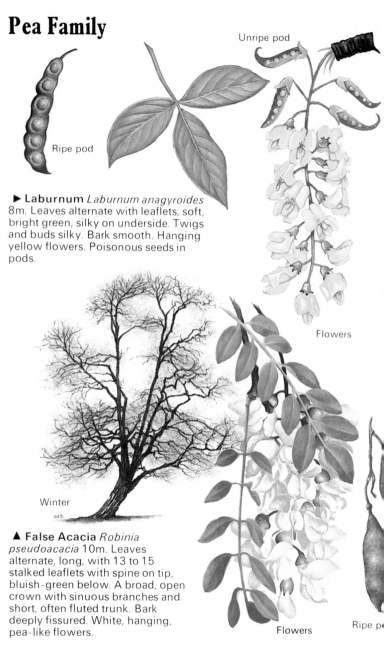

Ripe pod

Unripe pod

▶ **Laburnum** *Laburnum anagyroides*
8m. Leaves alternate with leaflets, soft,
bright green, silky on underside. Twigs
and buds silky. Bark smooth. Hanging
yellow flowers. Poisonous seeds in
pods.

Flowers

Winter

▲ **False Acacia** *Robinia
pseudoacacia* 10m. Leaves
alternate, long, with 13 to 15
stalked leaflets with spine on tip,
bluish-green below. A broad, open
crown with sinuous branches and
short, often fluted trunk. Bark
deeply fissured. White, hanging,
pea-like flowers.

Flowers

Ripe po

Elder, Holly and Olive

▶ **Elder** *Sambucus nigra* 9m. Leaves opposite with 5 to 7 leaflets, margins toothed. More often a bush than a tree. Light brown corky bark. Heads of numerous, creamy-white flowers with a heavy, sweet smell. Common on rough ground.

Ripe fruit

◀ **Holly** *Ilex aquifolium* 10m. Alternate, thick, shiny evergreen leaves with sharp spines. Bark smooth, green at first, warty and silver-grey later. Separate male and female trees. Flowers on both are small, clustered and greenish-white. Dense bunches of red berries occur on female trees. Common everywhere.

▶ **Olive** *Olea europaea* 10m. Long, opposite evergreen leaves, silvery-grey. A small, rounded tree with twisted branches and trunk. Small white flowers. Few trees flower in Britain. The rounded fleshy green fruit is oily; it ripens black and is edible. Mediterranean. Only planted in southern Britain, where fruit does not ripen.

Unripe fruit

Ripe fruit

Wild Flowers

Flowers are separated into families by their structure, which can be complicated and highly specialized. The flowers in the buttercup family *Ranunculaceae* are examples of the simplest type. An outer ring of greenish-yellow sepals surrounds the bright yellow petals, which are all similar in size and shape. The flower contains both male and female parts. The male parts are the numerous stamens with anthers bearing pollen, the female, the many ovaries each with a style and stigma. Such a flower is called a regular, perfect flower. In contrast, some flowers have sepals which are highly coloured and indistinguishable from the petals. Sepals and petals may be joined at the base, forming tubes.

Flower

Flower stalk

Bract

Leaf

Leaf stalk

Leaf axil

Stipule

Stem

Root

External Features of a Flowering Plant

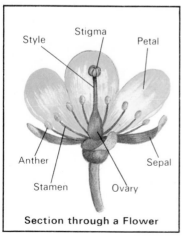

Style

Stigma

Petal

Anther

Stamen

Ovary

Sepal

Section through a Flower

As well as living in particular conditions, each plant often grows together with other species. Such associations of plants are called 'plant communities', and are typical of a particular climate and kind of soil. Some plants are short-lived (annuals and ephemerals), some take two years to mature (biennials), while others persist for many years, flowering every year (perennials).

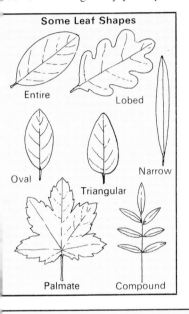

Some Leaf Shapes

Entire

Lobed

Oval

Narrow

Triangular

Palmate

Compound

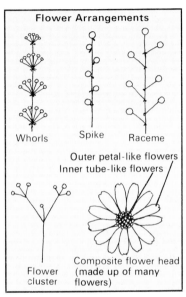

Flower Arrangements

Whorls

Spike

Raceme

Outer petal-like flowers
Inner tube-like flowers

Composite flower head (made up of many flowers)

Flower cluster

CLUES AND HINTS

Where to look: Wild flowers are everywhere, in towns as well as in the countryside.

Collecting flowers: Never dig up wild flowers, and do not pick a flower if you can only see a few of its kind. It might be very rare. You can pick the commoner flowers and press them, keeping a record of when and where found, the kind of soil and the height of the plant.

Leaf shape (see above): Look carefully at the shape of the leaf, whether it is entire or lobed, and its veining, as well as the way the leaves are arranged on the stem.

Flower arrangement (see above): Count the number of petals and notice the arrangement of flowers on the stem, whether solitary or in whorls, spikes, racemes, clusters or heads.

Buttercups

▶ **Meadow Buttercup** *Ranunculus acris* Up to 100cm. 5 bright, glossy, yellow, rounded petals, 5 green sepals. Common in grassland. Flowers April to October.

▲ **Lesser Spearwort** *Ranunculus flammula* 8–50cm. Leaves oval or long and narrow. Stem thick. 5 small petals. Common in wet places. Flowers May to September.

▶ **Lesser Celandine** *Ranunculus ficaria* 10–25cm. Single flowers on stem, 8 to 12 bright yellow petals, long and narrow. Leaves spade-shaped. Woods and hedge banks. Flowers early spring.

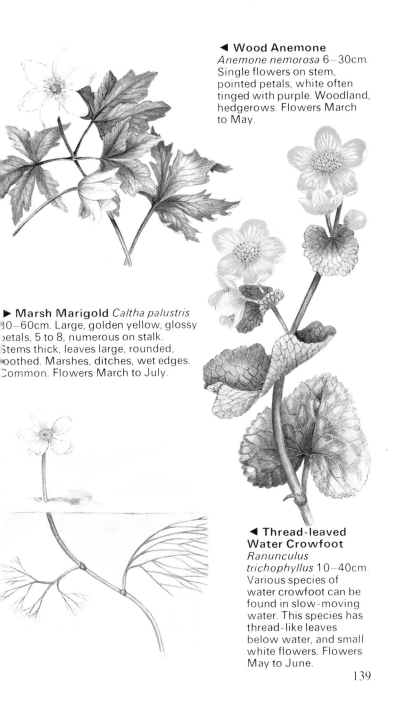

◀ Wood Anemone
Anemone nemorosa 6–30cm.
Single flowers on stem,
pointed petals, white often
tinged with purple. Woodland,
hedgerows. Flowers March
to May.

▶ Marsh Marigold *Caltha palustris*
30–60cm. Large, golden yellow, glossy
petals, 5 to 8, numerous on stalk.
Stems thick, leaves large, rounded,
toothed. Marshes, ditches, wet edges.
Common. Flowers March to July.

**◀ Thread-leaved
Water Crowfoot**
*Ranunculus
trichophyllus* 10–40cm.
Various species of
water crowfoot can be
found in slow-moving
water. This species has
thread-like leaves
below water, and small
white flowers. Flowers
May to June.

139

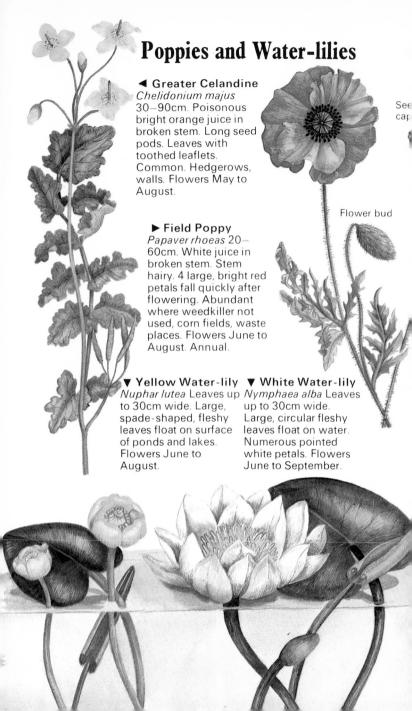

Poppies and Water-lilies

◄ Greater Celandine
Chelidonium majus
30–90cm. Poisonous
bright orange juice in
broken stem. Long seed
pods. Leaves with
toothed leaflets.
Common. Hedgerows,
walls. Flowers May to
August.

Seed
cap

Flower bud

► Field Poppy
Papaver rhoeas 20–
60cm. White juice in
broken stem. Stem
hairy. 4 large, bright red
petals fall quickly after
flowering. Abundant
where weedkiller not
used, corn fields, waste
places. Flowers June to
August. Annual.

▼ Yellow Water-lily
Nuphar lutea Leaves up
to 30cm wide. Large,
spade-shaped, fleshy
leaves float on surface
of ponds and lakes.
Flowers June to
August.

▼ White Water-lily
Nymphaea alba Leaves
up to 30cm wide.
Large, circular fleshy
leaves float on water.
Numerous pointed
white petals. Flowers
June to September.

Fumitory and Cabbage Family

▶ **Common Fumitory** *Fumaria officinalis* Up to 60cm. Pale green, finely divided leaves, feathery. Flowers in misty purple spikes. Each small flower has 4 pink, dark-tipped petals. Common arable fields and waste ground. Flowers May to October.

▲ **Lady's Smock** *Cardamine pratensis* 30–60cm. Flowers in groups, 4 pale purple petals. Damp meadows. Flowers April to June.

◀ **Wild Radish** *Raphanus raphanistrum* 20–60cm. Seed pod long. Leaves lobed. Waste places. Flowers May to September.

▶ **Shepherd's Purse** *Capsella bursa-pastoris* Up to 50cm. Seed pods small, heart-shaped. Leaves with deep lobes, mainly at base. Waste places. Flowers all year.

Violets, Milkwort and St John's Wort

▼ **Sweet Violet** *Viola odorata* 5–10cm. Flowers sweet-scented. 5 petals, the lowest with a pouch-like spur at base. Leaves rounded, heart-shaped. Hedge banks. Flowers February to April.

Seed capsule

White form

▲ **Wild Pansy** *Viola tricolor* 10–30cm. Upper petals purple, lower yellow with dark lines. Several flowers on a stem. Cultivated and grassy places. Flowers April to September.

▼ **Common Milkwort** *Polygala vulgaris* 10–30cm. Weak spreading stems. Small, flat flowers. Heaths and short grassland. Flowers May to September.

▶ **Common St John's Wort** *Hypericum perforatum* 30–90cm. Flower pale yellow, 5 petals with black dots on edges. Leaves opposite, dotted with glands. Stalk woody with raised lines. Common in grassland, hedgerows. Flowers June to September.

Stitchworts

▶ **Red Campion** *Silene vioica* 30–90cm. Leaves opposite, pointed and hairy. The 5 petals are heart-shaped at end. The green sepals form a ridged tube with 5 teeth at top. 10 stamens. Shady, damp woods and hedge banks. Flowers May to June.

◀ **Ragged Robin** *Lychnis flos-cuculi* 30–75cm. Leaves opposite. 5 pale pink petals, deeply divided into four. Sepals form a tube. 10 stamens. Wet meadows. Flowers May to June.

Flower

▶ **Common Mouse-ear Chickweed** *Cerastium holosteoides* 5cm. Leaves small, oval, very hairy. Flowers have 5 white petals with heart-shaped ends. Sepals only a little shorter so that flower is almost hidden. Waste places. Flowers April to September.

143

Stitchworts

◀ **Greater Stitchwort** *Stellaria holostea* 15—60cm. Weak, slender stem with 4 sides. 5 white, heart-shaped petals. Common in woods, hedgerows. Flowers April to June.

▶ **Corn Spurrey** *Spergula arvensis* 7—40cm. Trailing stems, leaves long and thread-like. Stem and leaves sticky due to hairs. Cornfields and waste places. Flowers June to August.

▶ **Common Chickweed** *Stellaria media* 5—40cm. Straggling leafy stems. 5 deeply divided white petals. Reddish stamens. Common gardens and waste places. Flowers all year.

Goosefoot, Mallow and Wood Sorrel

◄ **Fat Hen**
Chenopodium album
30–50cm. This member
of the goosefoot family
has numerous small,
green flowers in dense
bunches. Leaves
toothed and thick with
hairs giving the plant a
'mealy' appearance.
Waste places. Common.
Flowers July to
October.

Flower

▼ **Common Mallow** *Malva
sylvestris* 45–90cm. 5 purple
or white petals with darker
stripes. Heart-shaped at tip,
narrowing to base. Leaves
hairy with 5 to 7 triangular-
shaped lobes. Common on
roadsides. Flowers June to
September.

◄ **Wood Sorrel** *Oxalis
acetosella* 10–15cm. Leaves
clover-like on long slender
stalks. Single flower on stem,
with 5 rounded petals. Woods
especially oak and beech, in
shade. Flowers April to May.

145

Geraniums and Balsam

► **Meadow Cranesbill**
Geranium pratense 30–40cm.
Blue flowers have 5 petals
with rounded ends. Seed pods
have long pointed ends from
which the name comes.
Flowers June to September.

◄ **Herb Robert** *Geranium
robertianum* 10–50cm. Stem often
red, hairy. Plant has a characteristic
musty smell. 5 pinkish petals. Stamens
coloured orange by pollen. Seed pods
have thin beak. Common. Hedgerows
and woodland. Flowers May to
September.

► **Policeman's Helmet or Indian
Balsam** *Impatiens glandulifera* 1–2m.
Tall, succulent plant, with large,
distinctive purple flowers hanging on
thin stalks. Introduced from the
Himalayas. Common. River banks and
waste places. Flowers July to October.

Pea Family

◄ **Gorse** *Ulex europaeus* 60–200cm. Large, dense, prickly bush. Seed in pea-like pod, can be heard popping on hot days. Common. Heaths, moorland. Flowers mainly in late winter and spring.

Flower

▼ **Broom** *Sarothamnus scopasius* 60–200cm. Flowers similar in shape and colour to gorse. Has no spines. The twigs are woody and angled. Sandy heaths. Flowers May to June.

Flower

Seed pod

◄ **Bird's Foot Trefoil** *Lotus corniculatus* 10–40cm. Flowers pea-like. Buds red before opening. Seed pods are long and narrow. Grassy places. Flowers June to September.

147

Pea Family

▲**White Clover** *Trifolium repens*
20–40cm. Creeping stem,
but numerous small white flowers in
head. Flowers June to September.

◀**Red Clover** *Trifolium pratense*
50–60cm. Dense round heads
of small pea-like flowers, pinkish-
purple in colour. Grassy and cultivated
places. Flowers May to September.

▶ **Restharrow** *Ononis
repens* 30–60cm. Flowers
pea-like, rose-red with dark
stripes. Grassy places
especially on chalk. Flowers
June to September.

◀ **Tufted Vetch** *Vicia
cracca* 60–200cm. Numerous
leaflets with tendrils at end
which twine round other
vegetation for support.
Flowers pea-like in dense
heads. Hedgerows. Flowers
June to August.

148

Rose Family

◀ **Dog Rose** *Rosa canina* 1–3m. Long arching stems with many long, curved, sharp prickles. Leaves have 4 to 6 toothed leaflets; with leafy stipules attached to base of leaf stalk. Flowers showy, large with five heart-shaped pinkish petals which fall quickly. Numerous yellow stamens. The 5 green sepals turn back after flowering and fall before the fruit (round red, fleshy 'hip') is ripe. Flowers in hedgerows, June to July. Many other species of wild rose can be found growing in hedgerows and scrub.

▼ **Wild Strawberry** *Fragaria vesca* 5–30cm. Leaves are in tufts. Long runners are produced which root and form new plants. Woodland. Flowers April to July.

▲ **Bramble** *Rubus
fruticosus* Long, rambling,
woody stems with thorns.
Flowers are white or tinged
with pink. The 5 petals are
separated from each other.
5 pointed sepals, often turned
back. Fruit is the well-known
blackberry. Hedgerows,
woods. Flowers May to
September.

◀ **Meadowsweet**
Filipendula ulmaria
60–120cm. Creamy-
white heads of small
flowers. Leaves, 5 to 9
leaflets, covered with
whitish hairs below.
Reddish stems. Marshes
and wet grassland.
Flowers June to
September.

Rose Family and Stonecrop

► **Water Avens** *Geum rivale* 20–60cm. The nodding flowers have 5 long sepals alternating with 5 shorter ones. 5 pinkish-orange petals and numerous yellow stamens. Leaves 7 to 13 leaflets, the end one rounded, lobed and toothed. Marshy places. Flowers May to September. Wood avens *Geum urbanum* similar to water avens but with yellow flowers.

Flower

◄ **Silverweed** *Potentilla anserina* Up to 80cm. Leaves in rosettes on long runners which root at intervals. Green above, covered with dense, silvery-white hairs below. Flower has long, often red stalk. 5 round yellow petals. Waste places. Flowers June to August. Another species, tormentil *Potentilla erecta*, has yellow flowers with 4 petals.

► **Biting Stonecrop** *Sedum acre* 2–10cm. Small, round, fleshy leaves crowded together, often forming dense mats. Flowers bright yellow. Walls, dry grassland. Flowers June to July.

151

Saxifrage, Grass of Parnassus, Loosestrife and Sundew

◄ Rue-leaved Saxifrage
Saxifraga tridactylites 2–15cm. Small white flowers with 5 petals. Leaves grow from rosette at ground level. Dry places. Flowers April to June.

► Grass of Parnassus *Parnassia palustris* 10–30cm. Large, single white flower with 5 rounded, green-veined petals. Wet meadows, uplands. Flowers July to October.

◄ Purple Loosestrife
Lythrum salicaria 60–120cm. Flowers in whorls on dense, long, purple spikes. Margins of lakes and ponds. Flowers June to August.

► Sundew *Drosera rotundifolia* 6–25cm. Rosettes of round leaves covered with red sticky glands for catching flies. Bogs, wet places. Flowers June to August.

Willowherbs and Ivy

Flower

◀ **Enchanter's Nightshade** *Circaea lutetiana* 30–60cm. Flowers in loose heads, 2 pinkish-white, lobed petals. Seed has hooked hairs attaching it to the fur or hair of animals. Moist and shady woods, waste ground. Flowers June to August.

▶ **Rosebay Willowherb** *Epilobium angustifolium* Up to 120cm. Leaves long, narrow with raised mid vein. Flowers in long spikes tapering to point. Woolly seeds. Bare ground. Flowers July to September.

Flower

Seeds

◀ **Ivy** *Hedera helix* Climbs to 30m. Long, trailing woody stems. Clings to walls and trees and also creeps on ground. Evergreen. Flowers September to November.

Fruit cluster

153

Carrot Family

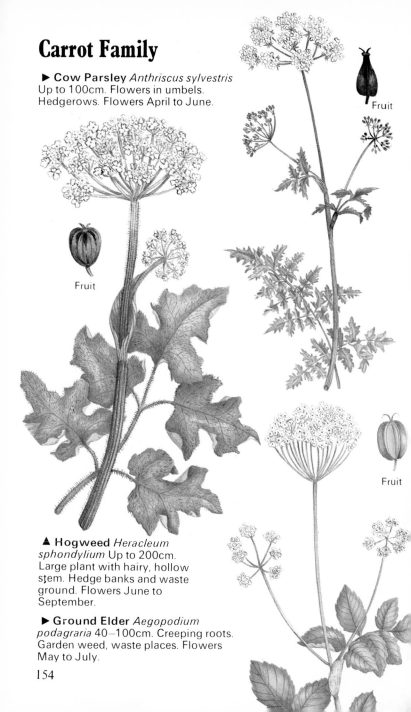

▶ **Cow Parsley** *Anthriscus sylvestris*
Up to 100cm. Flowers in umbels.
Hedgerows. Flowers April to June.

Fruit

Fruit

▲ **Hogweed** *Heracleum
sphondylium* Up to 200cm.
Large plant with hairy, hollow
stem. Hedge banks and waste
ground. Flowers June to
September.

Fruit

▶ **Ground Elder** *Aegopodium
podagraria* 40–100cm. Creeping roots.
Garden weed, waste places. Flowers
May to July.

Spurge and Docks

◀ **Dog's Mercury** *Mercurialis perennis* 15–40cm. This spurge has many flowers in green spikes. Male and female flowers separate. Woodland. Flowers February to April.

◀ **Redshank** *Polygonum persicaria* 25–75cm. Stems purplish or red. Leaves long and pointed. Many flowers in compact, dense pink head. Arable fields and waste places. Flowers June to October.

Fruit

◀ **Common Sorrel** *Rumex acetosa* Up to 100cm. Flowers green in loose heads. Male and female flowers on different plants. Seeds green with red edges. Grassland. Flowers May to July.

▶ **Broad-leaved Dock** *Rumex obtusifolius* 50–100cm. Green and red flowers in whorls up stem. Fields, waste ground. Weed in pasture. Flowers June to October.

Fruit

Nettle, Heather and Thrift

◄ **Nettle** *Urtica dioica* 30–150cm. Leaves opposite with sharp teeth and sharp stinging hairs. Flowers hang in long spikes. Male and female on separate plants. Flowers June to August.

► **Heather** *Calluna vulgaris* Up to 60cm. Evergreen leaves are small, needle-like and opposite. 4 petals and 4 sepals coloured pale purple, sometimes white. Flower in loose spikes. Heaths and moors. Flowers July to September.

► **Bilberry** *Vaccinium myrtillus* 60cm. Leaves small, oval. Fruit round, ripening black. Heaths, moors. Flowers April to June.

◄ **Thrift** *Armeria maritima* 5–20cm. Long, thin leaves form clumps. Flowers rosy-pink in round head. Sepals form tube. Coastal marshes, cliffs. Also on mountains inland. Flowers April to October.

Primroses and Gentians

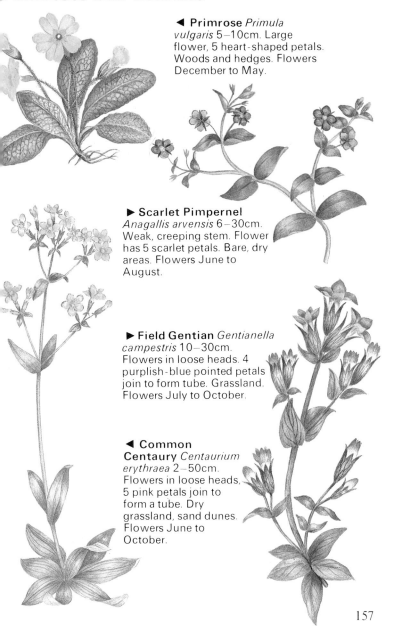

◄ **Primrose** *Primula vulgaris* 5–10cm. Large flower, 5 heart-shaped petals. Woods and hedges. Flowers December to May.

► **Scarlet Pimpernel** *Anagallis arvensis* 6–30cm. Weak, creeping stem. Flower has 5 scarlet petals. Bare, dry areas. Flowers June to August.

► **Field Gentian** *Gentianella campestris* 10–30cm. Flowers in loose heads. 4 purplish-blue pointed petals join to form tube. Grassland. Flowers July to October.

◄ **Common Centaury** *Centaurium erythraea* 2–50cm. Flowers in loose heads, 5 pink petals join to form a tube. Dry grassland, sand dunes. Flowers June to October.

Borage Family

Flower

◀ **Field Forget-me-not**
Myosotis arvensis 15–30cm.
5 bright blue petals, yellow
centre. Roadsides, bare
places. Flowers April to
September.

▶ **Viper's Bugloss**
Echium vulgare 30–
90cm. Flower is pink in
bud, opening to blue. 5
stamens, 4 of which
project beyond flower
with the forked stigma.
Roadsides, dry places.
Flowers June to
September.

Colour
variants

◀ **Common Comfrey**
Symphytum officinale 30–
120cm. Very rough, hairy
plant. Large, pointed leaf
encloses the stem at base.
Many flowers in drooping
heads. Stigma projects
beyond the flower. Damp and
waste places. Flowers May
to June.

Bogbean, Bindweed and Nightshades

▶ **Bogbean** *Menyanthes trifoliata* 15–30cm. Fresh water, damp edges, stems often floating. Flowers May to July.

▼ **Bindweed** *Calystegia sepium* 20–75cm. Climbing stems twine round other plants. Common hedges, waste places. Weed in gardens. Flowers July to September.

▼ **Deadly Nightshade** *Atropa bella-donna* 150cm. Berry black, poisonous. In scrub on chalk soils. Flowers June to August.

Berries

▶ **Bittersweet** *Solanum dulcamara* 30–200cm. 5 narrow, sharply-pointed purple petals. Berries red. Leaves oval with sharp point. Woods, waste ground. Flowers June to September.

159

Figworts

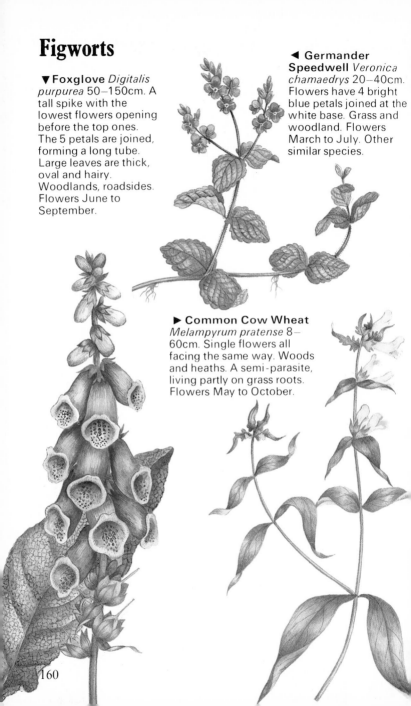

▼ **Foxglove** *Digitalis purpurea* 50–150cm. A tall spike with the lowest flowers opening before the top ones. The 5 petals are joined, forming a long tube. Large leaves are thick, oval and hairy. Woodlands, roadsides. Flowers June to September.

◄ **Germander Speedwell** *Veronica chamaedrys* 20–40cm. Flowers have 4 bright blue petals joined at the white base. Grass and woodland. Flowers March to July. Other similar species.

► **Common Cow Wheat** *Melampyrum pratense* 8–60cm. Single flowers all facing the same way. Woods and heaths. A semi-parasite, living partly on grass roots. Flowers May to October.

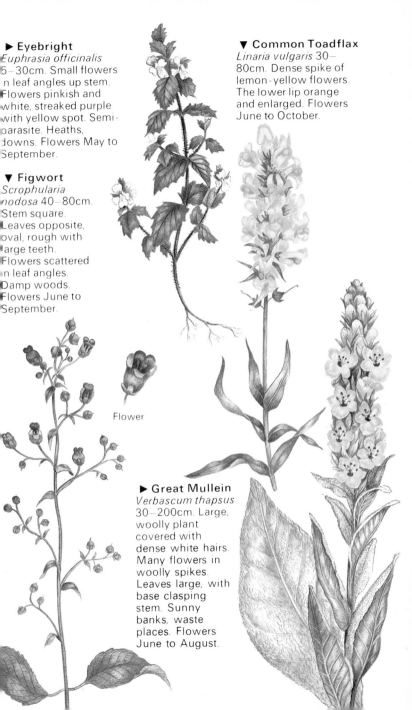

▶ Eyebright
Euphrasia officinalis
5–30cm. Small flowers
in leaf angles up stem.
Flowers pinkish and
white, streaked purple
with yellow spot. Semi-
parasite. Heaths,
downs. Flowers May to
September.

▼ Figwort
*Scrophularia
nodosa* 40–80cm.
Stem square.
Leaves opposite,
oval, rough with
large teeth.
Flowers scattered
in leaf angles.
Damp woods.
Flowers June to
September.

Flower

▼ Common Toadflax
Linaria vulgaris 30–
80cm. Dense spike of
lemon-yellow flowers.
The lower lip orange
and enlarged. Flowers
June to October.

▶ Great Mullein
Verbascum thapsus
30–200cm. Large,
woolly plant
covered with
dense white hairs.
Many flowers in
woolly spikes.
Leaves large, with
base clasping
stem. Sunny
banks, waste
places. Flowers
June to August.

Mints, Plantain and Bellflower

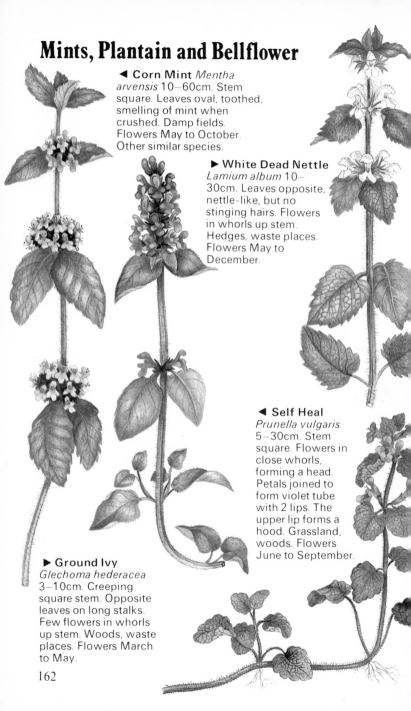

◀ **Corn Mint** *Mentha arvensis* 10–60cm. Stem square. Leaves oval, toothed, smelling of mint when crushed. Damp fields. Flowers May to October. Other similar species.

▶ **White Dead Nettle** *Lamium album* 10–30cm. Leaves opposite, nettle-like, but no stinging hairs. Flowers in whorls up stem. Hedges, waste places. Flowers May to December.

◀ **Self Heal** *Prunella vulgaris* 5–30cm. Stem square. Flowers in close whorls, forming a head. Petals joined to form violet tube with 2 lips. The upper lip forms a hood. Grassland, woods. Flowers June to September.

▶ **Ground Ivy** *Glechoma hederacea* 3–10cm. Creeping square stem. Opposite leaves on long stalks. Few flowers in whorls up stem. Woods, waste places. Flowers March to May.

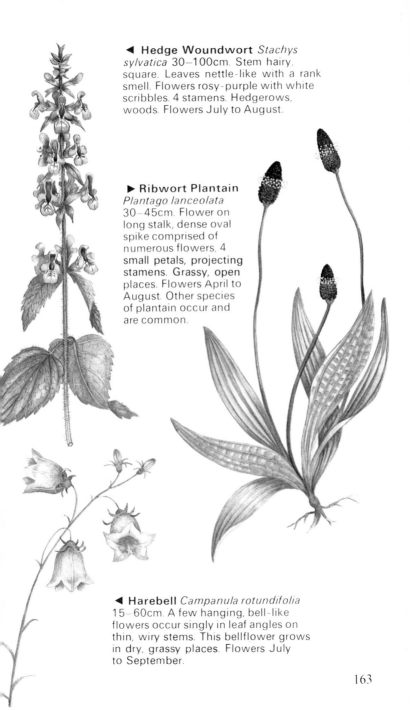

◀ **Hedge Woundwort** *Stachys sylvatica* 30–100cm. Stem hairy, square. Leaves nettle-like with a rank smell. Flowers rosy-purple with white scribbles. 4 stamens. Hedgerows, woods. Flowers July to August.

▶ **Ribwort Plantain** *Plantago lanceolata* 30–45cm. Flower on long stalk, dense oval spike comprised of numerous flowers. 4 small petals, projecting stamens. Grassy, open places. Flowers April to August. Other species of plantain occur and are common.

◀ **Harebell** *Campanula rotundifolia* 15–60cm. A few hanging, bell-like flowers occur singly in leaf angles on thin, wiry stems. This bellflower grows in dry, grassy places. Flowers July to September.

163

Bedstraws and Honeysuckle

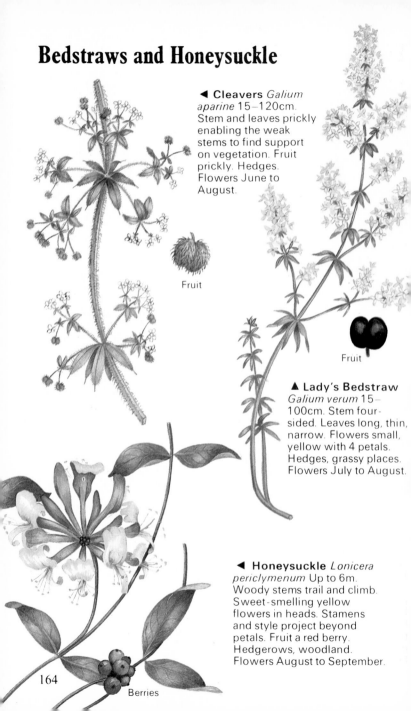

◀ **Cleavers** *Galium aparine* 15–120cm. Stem and leaves prickly enabling the weak stems to find support on vegetation. Fruit prickly. Hedges. Flowers June to August.

Fruit

Fruit

▲ **Lady's Bedstraw** *Galium verum* 15–100cm. Stem four-sided. Leaves long, thin, narrow. Flowers small, yellow with 4 petals. Hedges, grassy places. Flowers July to August.

◀ **Honeysuckle** *Lonicera periclymenum* Up to 6m. Woody stems trail and climb. Sweet-smelling yellow flowers in heads. Stamens and style project beyond petals. Fruit a red berry. Hedgerows, woodland. Flowers August to September.

Berries

Teasels and Valerian

▶ **Field Scabious** *Knautia arvensis*
(far right) 25–100cm. Flowers
numerous in dense head, the largest on
the outside. Purple, with 4 unequal
lilac-blue petals. Dry grassland.
Flowers July to September.

▶ **Devil's Bit Scabious**
Succisa pratense 15–100cm.
Root short, thick, ending as if
bitten off. Flowers in dense
head, all the same size.
Flowers have 4 petals, 4
stamens. Grassland, woods.
Flowers June to October.

wer

▲ **Common Valerian**
Valeriana officinalis 20–
150cm. Numerous small pale
pink flowers in dense heads.
Leaves divided into many-
lobed leaflets, narrower on
the stem. Earthy smell. Grassy
places and wood edges.
Flowers June to August.

Daisy Family

▶ **Daisy** *Bellis perennis* 2–8cm. Numerous flowers in what seems to be a single head. Outer ones long, white, petal-like, sometimes pink-tipped. Inner flowers short, tubular, yellow, forming centre or disc. Grassland. Flowers March to October. Ox eye daisy *Chrysanthemum leucanthemum* 50cm. Similar. Larger.

▼ **Scentless Mayweed** *Matricaria maritima* 10–30cm. Feathery-looking foliage. Single flower heads on stem. Outer flowers white, narrow, petal-like. Inner flowers short tubes forming a yellow dome in 'flower centre'. Bare ground. Flowers July to September.

▼ **Sea Aster** *Aster tripolium* 15–100cm. Stem and leaves fleshy. Leaves long, narrow. Grows on salt marshes by sea. Flowers July to October.

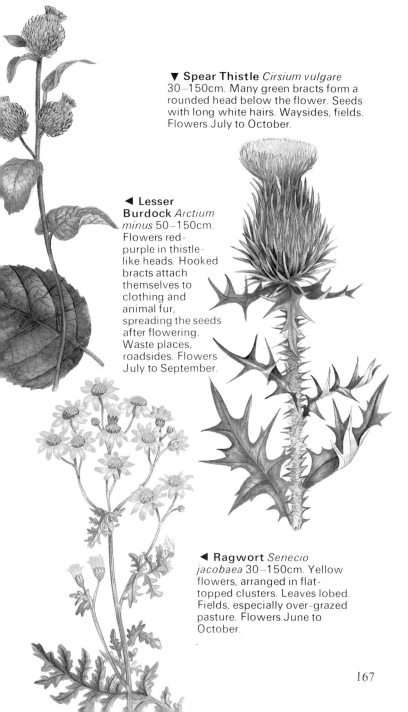

▼ Spear Thistle *Cirsium vulgare*
30–150cm. Many green bracts form a
rounded head below the flower. Seeds
with long white hairs. Waysides, fields.
Flowers July to October.

**◀ Lesser
Burdock** *Arctium
minus* 50–150cm.
Flowers red-
purple in thistle-
like heads. Hooked
bracts attach
themselves to
clothing and
animal fur,
spreading the seeds
after flowering.
Waste places,
roadsides. Flowers
July to September.

◀ Ragwort *Senecio
jacobaea* 30–150cm. Yellow
flowers, arranged in flat-
topped clusters. Leaves lobed.
Fields, especially over-grazed
pasture. Flowers June to
October.

Daisy Family

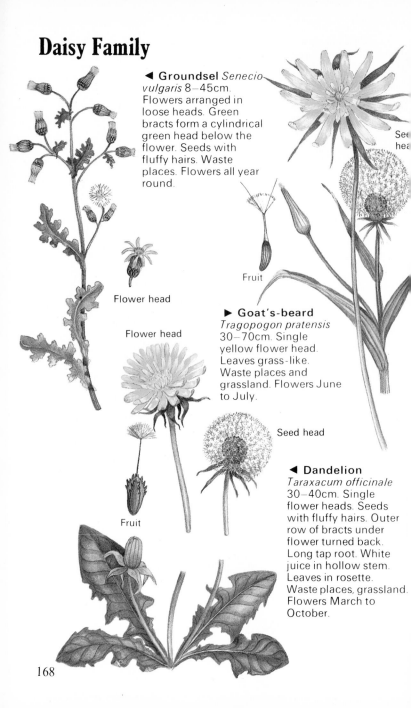

◄ **Groundsel** *Senecio vulgaris* 8–45cm. Flowers arranged in loose heads. Green bracts form a cylindrical green head below the flower. Seeds with fluffy hairs. Waste places. Flowers all year round.

Seed head

Fruit

Flower head

Flower head

► **Goat's-beard** *Tragopogon pratensis* 30–70cm. Single yellow flower head. Leaves grass-like. Waste places and grassland. Flowers June to July.

Seed head

Fruit

◄ **Dandelion** *Taraxacum officinale* 30–40cm. Single flower heads. Seeds with fluffy hairs. Outer row of bracts under flower turned back. Long tap root. White juice in hollow stem. Leaves in rosette. Waste places, grassland. Flowers March to October.

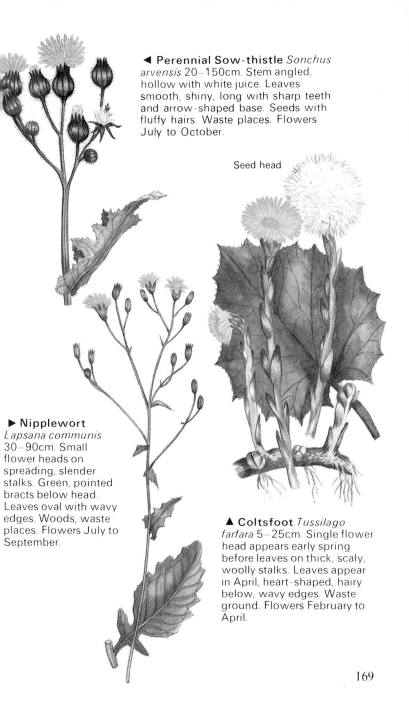

◄ **Perennial Sow-thistle** *Sonchus arvensis* 20–150cm. Stem angled, hollow with white juice. Leaves smooth, shiny, long with sharp teeth and arrow-shaped base. Seeds with fluffy hairs. Waste places. Flowers July to October.

Seed head

► **Nipplewort**
Lapsana communis
30–90cm. Small flower heads on spreading, slender stalks. Green, pointed bracts below head. Leaves oval with wavy edges. Woods, waste places. Flowers July to September.

▲ **Coltsfoot** *Tussilago farfara* 5–25cm. Single flower head appears early spring before leaves on thick, scaly, woolly stalks. Leaves appear in April, heart-shaped, hairy below, wavy edges. Waste ground. Flowers February to April.

Flower head

Daisy Family

◀ **Butterbur** *Petasites hybridus* Up to 150cm. Flowers appear before the leaves in a compact spike. Leaves large and heart-shaped like coltsfoot, but grey hairs below. Wet and damp meadows, river banks, ditches. Flowers March to May.

▼ **Hemp Agrimony** *Eupatorium cannabinum* 30–120cm. Flower heads in rather loose, domed clusters. Opposite leaves, almost stalkless. Marshes, stream sides. Flowers July to September.

▼ **Yarrow** *Achillea millefolium* 5–15cm. Flowers arranged in flat-topped clusters. Leaves have deeply divided leaflets giving feathery appearance. Meadows, pastures. Flowers June to August.

Flower head

Lilies and Arum

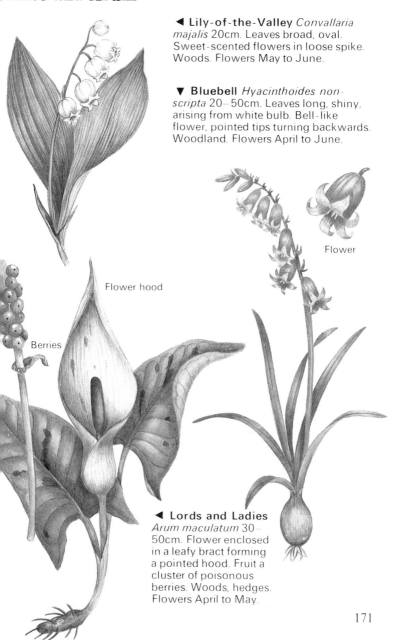

◀ **Lily-of-the-Valley** *Convallaria majalis* 20cm. Leaves broad, oval. Sweet-scented flowers in loose spike. Woods. Flowers May to June.

▼ **Bluebell** *Hyacinthoides nonscripta* 20–50cm. Leaves long, shiny, arising from white bulb. Bell-like flower, pointed tips turning backwards. Woodland. Flowers April to June.

Flower

Flower hood

Berries

◀ **Lords and Ladies** *Arum maculatum* 30–50cm. Flower enclosed in a leafy bract forming a pointed hood. Fruit a cluster of poisonous berries. Woods, hedges. Flowers April to May.

171

Iris and Daffodils

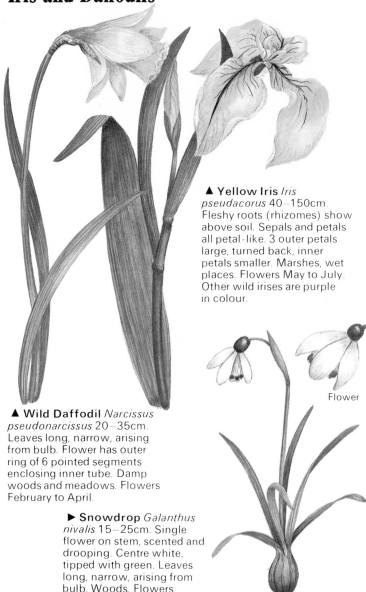

▲ **Yellow Iris** *Iris pseudacorus* 40–150cm. Fleshy roots (rhizomes) show above soil. Sepals and petals all petal-like. 3 outer petals large, turned back, inner petals smaller. Marshes, wet places. Flowers May to July. Other wild irises are purple in colour.

Flower

▲ **Wild Daffodil** *Narcissus pseudonarcissus* 20–35cm. Leaves long, narrow, arising from bulb. Flower has outer ring of 6 pointed segments enclosing inner tube. Damp woods and meadows. Flowers February to April.

▶ **Snowdrop** *Galanthus nivalis* 15–25cm. Single flower on stem, scented and drooping. Centre white, tipped with green. Leaves long, narrow, arising from bulb. Woods. Flowers January to March.

Orchids

▶ **Early Purple Orchid** *Orchis mascula* 15–60cm. Many purple flowers in a loose spike. Leaves oval with bases enfolding the stem. Heavily blotched with black spots. Pastures, woods on chalky soils. Flowers April to June.

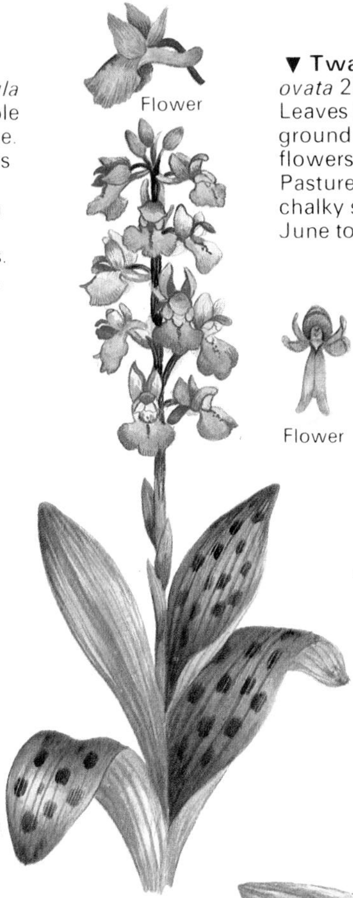

Flower

▼ **Twayblade** *Listera ovata* 20–60cm. Leaves in pairs at ground level. Many flowers in loose spike. Pasture, woods on chalky soils. Flowers June to July.

Flower

Flower

◀ **Broad-leaved Helleborine** *Epipactis helleborine* 15–50cm. Flowers in spikes. Sepals and petals green or purple. Woods. Flowers July to August.

Rhizome

173

Mushrooms and Toadstools

Mushrooms and toadstools are the fruit bodies of fungi that consist mainly of white strands in the soil or under the bark or in the wood of trees. These fruit bodies appear only when the fungus is ready to produce spores which are simple 'seeds'. Their function is to carry the spores above the ground so that they will be carried by air currents to new places. There are many different kinds of fungus fruit bodies, but the most commonly seen have a cap which opens out to expose gills or tubes (pores) underneath. These produce large quantities of minute spores. The cap is borne on a stalk and there may be a ring at the top of the stalk where the cap has broken away from it to open. Most fungi produce fruit bodies in the autumn, so September and October are the best months to look for them.

External Features of Fungus Fruit Body with Gills

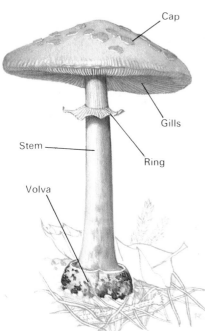

Cap

Gills

Stem

Ring

Volva

CLUES AND HINTS

Where to look: The edges of woodlands and fields are particularly good places to look for a wide variety of species.

Poison: Never pick or eat a mushroom until you are absolutely certain that it is not poisonous.

▼ **Beefsteak Fungus** *Fistulina hepatica* 5–30cm. Red-brown, hoof-shaped, growing rapidly in late summer on oak trees.

Fungi with Gills

◄ **Fly Agaric** *Amanita muscaria* Cap 6–16cm, red with white patches. Gills white. Stem white with ring and bulbous base. Occurs in birch woods. POISONOUS.

▶ **Death Cap** *Amanita phalloides* Cap 7–12cm, olive or yellowish-green and indistinctly streaky. Gills white. Stem white or yellow-green with ring and cup-like volva at base. Found in leafy woods, especially with oak. Extremely POISONOUS, usually fatal.

▶ **Tawny Grisette** *Amanitopsis fulva* Cap 4–7cm, orange or tawny, acorn-shaped then flat with raised, darker centre, and piecrust edge. Gills white. Stem tall, fragile with sack-like volva but no ring. Woodlands. Edible.

▼ **Parasol Mushroom** *Lepiota procera* Cap 10–20cm, becoming flat with central boss. Gills white. Stem tall with ring. Broadleaved woodland clearings and pastures. Edible.

◄ **Shaggy Parasol** *Lepiota rhacodes* Cap 8–15cm. Like parasol mushroom but shorter, sturdy, lacks scales on stem and cut flesh turns red. Central boss flattened. Shady woods and gardens. Edible.

175

Fungi with Gills

◄ **Poached Egg Fungus** *Oudemansiella mucida* Cap 3–8cm, slimy, white or with greyish tint. Gills widely spaced and white. Stem thin, firm, with ring. Clustered on trunks of dead and dying beech trees in autumn. Edible but not recommended.

▲ **Honey Fungus** *Armillaria mellea* Cap 3–10cm, tawny with darker scales. Stem honey-coloured with cottony ring. Gills whitish. Kills many trees and shrubs. Common. Edible when young.

◄ **Horn of Plenty** *Craterellus cornucopioides* Cap 9cm, hollow, funnel-shaped with wavy margin. Outside uneven, smoky-grey; inside felty, grey-brown. In clusters on ground. Edible.

► **Chanterelle** *Cantharellus cibarius* Cap 3–10cm, cone-shaped, apricot or egg-yellow. Gills irregularly branched, fold-like, running down stem. Broadleaved woods. Edible.

▶ **Saffron Milk Cap** *Lactarius deliciosus* Cap 4–10cm, concave, orange-red, staining green. Gills exuding carrot-coloured juice when broken. Under coniferous trees. Edible.

▼ **Ugly Milk Cap** *Lactarius turpis* Cap 6–14cm, olive-brown, margin yellowish. Gills yellow-brown, exuding white 'milk' when cut. Under birch trees. Inedible.

▶ **Clouded Agaric** *Clitocybe nebularis* Cap 6–15cm, flattened, ash-grey. Stem stout, lighter. Gills whitish. Occurs in woods. Indigestible.

◀ **The Sickener** *Russula emetica* Cap 6–9cm, shiny scarlet, becoming concave. Flesh peppery. Gills white. Under conifers and beech. Causes vomiting.

▶ **Velvet Shank** *Flammulina velutipes* Cap 2–6cm, yellowish, slimy. Stem dark brown velvety. Gills pale yellow. In winter on trunks and branches. Edible.

Fungi with Gills

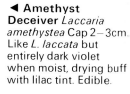

◄ Amethyst Deceiver *Laccaria amethystea* Cap 2–3cm. Like *L. laccata* but entirely dark violet when moist, drying buff with lilac tint. Edible.

▼ Spindle Shank *Collybia fusipes* Cap 3–8cm, reddish-brown or liver-coloured. Gills whitish, often spotted. Stem red-brown, grooved. Tufted at base of oak and beech. Edible.

▲ Wood Blewit *Lepista nuda*. At first entirely lilac or violet. Cap 6–10cm, becoming brownish with age. Gills crowded, violet, fading when old. Woods. Edible.

► Deceiver *Laccaria laccata* Cap 1–4cm. Cap and stem reddish-brown when moist, drying buff. Gills thick, uneven, flesh-coloured. Stem tough. Variable in form. Common. Edible.

◄ Fairy-ring Champignon *Marasmius oreades* Cap 2–6cm, pink, tan or buff, with central boss. Gills pale, widely spaced. In short grass; often in fairy rings. Edible.

▶ St George's Mushroom

Tricholoma gambosum
Cap 5–15cm, thick, fleshy, whitish. Gills white, crowded. Stem thick, swollen at base. Flesh has mealy smell. Amongst grass in spring. Edible.

▲ *Hygrophorus coccineus* (No common name) At first entirely scarlet, fading yellowish. Cap moist, 2–5cm, domed. Gills waxy. In grass. Edible.

▶ Milking Mycena

Mycena galopus Cap to 1.5cm, conical, grey with darker centre and radiating lines. Stem similar exuding white 'milk' when broken. Gills white. Amongst dead leaves in autumn. Inedible.

◀ Oyster Fungus

Pleurotus ostreatus
Cap 3–15cm, blue-grey then fawn, fan or shell-shaped. Attached at side by stalk. Gills whitish, running down stem. Edible but tough.

Fungi with Gills

◄ **Common Pluteus** *Pluteus cervinus* Cap 3–8cm, sooty brown or umber, becoming flattened. Gills pinkish, free. Stem white, streaked below with brown fibrils. Edible.

▼ *Gymnopilus junonius* (No common name) Cap 6–12cm, rounded, golden-brown, scaly. Stem similar with ring. Gills rust-coloured, crowded. Tufted at base of trunks. Inedible.

▼ *Pholiota aurivella* (No common name) Cap 5–12cm, glutinous, deep yellow with concentric chestnut scales. Stem light yellow with temporary ring and brown scales below. Gills becoming rust-coloured. Inedible.

▼ **Shaggy Pholiota** *Pholiota squarrosa* Cap 3–8cm, rounded, straw-coloured, densely covered with upturned scales. Stem similarly scaly. Edible, but very tough.

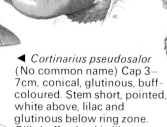

◄ *Cortinarius pseudosalor* (No common name) Cap 3–7cm, conical, glutinous, buff-coloured. Stem short, pointed, white above, lilac and glutinous below ring zone. Gills buff, edged in lilac. Edible.

◀ *Inocybe geophylla*
(No common name)
Cap 2cm, white, silky,
bell-shaped then
flattened with central
boss. Gills becoming
clay-brown. Stem
slender, white. Lilac
variety (right) *I.g.* var.
lilacina. POISONOUS.

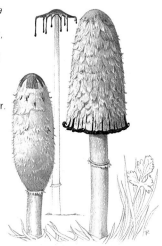

▼ **Field Mushroom** *Agaricus
campestris* Cap 4—8cm, smooth, white
or brownish. Stem short, slight ring.
Gills deep pink then purplish-brown.
Flesh white or brownish. Occurs in
fields. Edible.

▲ **Shaggy Ink Cap**
Coprinus comatus Cap
5—12cm long.
Cylindrical then bell-
shaped, white, shaggy.
Stem tall with ring.
Gills finally black and
dissolving into inky
fluid. Fields and rubbish
dumps. Edible.

◀ **Sulphur Tuft**
Hypholoma fasciculare
Cap 3—7cm, bright
sulphur yellow, centre
darker. Stem slender,
yellow, no ring. Gills
sulphur yellow,
becoming olive.
POISONOUS.

▶ **Verdigris Fungus**
Stropharia aeruginosa
Cap 2—8cm, blue-
green, slimy, convex,
flecked with white
scales. Stem stout,
paler, scaly below ring.
Inedible.

Fungi with Tubes

◀ *Suillus grevillei* (No common name) Cap 5–12cm, slimy, yellow. Stem darker with ring. Occurs in coniferous woods. Edible.

▶ **Orange Cap Boletus** *Leccinum versipelle* Cap 8–20cm, hemispherical, orange or brick-red. Stem robust with black dots. Found in pastures and woods. Edible.

▶ **Cep** *Boletus edulis* Cap 6–20cm, bun-like, warm brown. Stem swollen, pale brown with whitish network of veins. Pores white or yellow-green. Woodlands. Edible.

▼ **Dryad's Saddle** *Polyporus squamosus* Cap 10–30cm, fan-shaped, buff with brown scales. Stem off-centre. Edible.

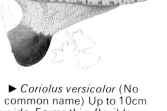

▲ **Birch Bracket** *Piptoporus betulinus* 10–20cm wide. Smooth, greyish, hoof-shaped. Confined to birch. Inedible.

▶ *Coriolus versicolor* (No common name) Up to 10cm wide. Forms thin, flexible, tiered brackets; upper surface velvety, zoned in shades of brown. Inedible.

Other Fungi

▶ *Hydnum repandum* (No common name) Cap 5–12cm, fleshy, convex, pinkish-buff with crowded spines beneath. Stem white. Deciduous woodlands. Edible.

◀ *Clavulina cristata* (No common name) 3–8cm high, forming branched, white, coral-like tufts. On ground in woods. Edible, but best avoided.

▼ **Jew's Ear** *Auricularia auricula-judae* 3–10cm. Helmet-shaped with ear-like folds beneath. Light brown, flabby and gelatinous with velvety surface. Edible.

▲ **Earth Star** *Geastrum triplex* Up to 10cm wide. Spore sac sitting in saucer-like portion. Deciduous woodland. Inedible.

▼ **Common Earth-ball** *Scleroderma citrinum* 4–8cm wide. Rounded, yellowish, scaly. Interior purplish-black. Found on sandy heaths and woodland. Inedible.

183

Index

(English Names)

Acacia, False 134
Adder 61
Admiral, Red 75
  White 75
Agaric, Clouded 177
  Fly 175
Agrimony, Hemp 170
Alder 5, 121
Alder fly 89
Almond 133
Amphibians 60, 62-63
Anemone, Beadlet 101
  Dahlia 101
Anemone, Wood 139
Ant, Black 86
  Dark 86
  Wood 86
Apple, Crab 132
Artemis, Rayed 98
Arthropods 72
Ash 103, 104, 130
  Manna 130
Aspen 118
Assassin bug 85
Aster, Sea 166
Auks 39
Avens, Water 151
Avocet 36

Badger 6, 8, 13
Barbel 69
Barnacle, Acorn 100
Bass 70
Bat, Daubenton's 18
  Greater horseshoe 18
  Long-eared 18
  Natterer's 18
  Noctule 18
  Whiskered 18
Bedstraw, Lady's 164
Bee, Bumblebee 4
  Cuckoo 86
  Honey 86
  Leafcutter 86
  Mining 86
  White-tailed
    bumblebee 86
Beech 103, 122
Bee-eater 42
Beefsteak fungus 174
Beetles 83-84
Bilberry 156
Bindweed 159
Birch bracket 182
Birds 20-59
Birds of prey 28-29
Bittern 23
Bittersweet 159

Bivalves 94, 95, 98
Blackbird 50
Blackcap 52
Blackfly 85
Blenny, Montagu's 71
Blewit, Wood 178
Bluebell 171
Bluebottle 88
Blue butterfly, Small 78
Bluethroat 51
Boar, Wild 17
Bogbean 159
Boletus, Orange cap 182
Bramble 150
Bream, Common 68
  Silver 68
Brimstone butterfly 74
Broadleaved trees 102,
  103, 118–135
Broom 147
Brown butterfly,
  Meadow 77
Buff ermine moth 80
Buff-tip moth 79
Bugloss, Viper's 158
Bugs 85
Bullfinch 20, 57
Bullhead 67
Bunting, Cirl 58
  Corn 58
  Ortolan 58
  Reed 59
  Rock 59
  Snow 58
Burdock, Lesser 167
Burnet,
  Six-spot 82
Burying beetle 83
Butterbur 170
Buttercup, Meadow 136,
  138
Butterflies 74–78
Buzzard 28

Caddis fly 89
Camberwell beauty 76
Campion, Red 143
Capercaillie 30
Cardinal beetle 84
Carp 68
Carrot family 154
Cedar, Atlas 106
  Japanese red 113
  of Lebanon 107
  Western red 115
Celandine, Greater 140
  Lesser 138
Centaury, Common 157
Centipede 92

Cep 182
Chaffinch 20, 21, 57
Chamois 7
Champignon, Fairy-ring
  178
Chanterelle 176
Chats 51
Cherry, Bird 133
  Wild 133
Chestnut, Horse 103, 128
  Sweet 123
Chickweed, Common 144
  Common Mouse-ear 143
Chiffchaff 53
Chile pine 116
Chinaman's hat 96
Chiton 94, 97
Chough 47
Chub 69
Cicada, Southern 85
Cinnabar moth 80
Clearwing moth,
  Hornet 82
Cleavers 164
Click beetle 83
Clouded yellow butterfly 74
Clover, Red 148
  White 148
Coastal fishes 70-71
Cockchafer 83
Cockle 98
  Dog 98
Cockroach 91
Cod 70
Codlin moth 82
Colorado beetle 84
Coltsfoot 169
Comfrey, Common 158
Comma butterfly 76
Conifers 102, 103, 105
Coot 32
Copper butterfly, Small 78
Cormorant 23
Corncrake 32
Cow parsley 154
Cowrie, European 97
Cow wheat, Common 160
Coypu 9
Crab 95
  Hermit 101
  Shore 101
Crake, Spotted 32
Crane 32
Cranesbill, Meadow 146
Crawfish 95
Cricket,
  Bush, Great green 91
  Field 91
  House 91
Crossbill 57

Crow, Carrion 20, 46
    Hooded 46
Crustaceans 95
Cuckoo 40
Curlew 20, 34
    Stone 36
Cuttlefish 101
Cypress, Italian 115
    Lawson 114
    Leyland 102, 114
    Monterey 114
    Swamp 113

Dab 70
Dace 68
Daffodil, Wild 172
Daisy family 166-170
Damselfly, Large red 90
Dandelion 168
Dead nettle, White 162
Death cap 175
Death watch beetle 84
Deceiver 178
    Amethyst 178
Deciduous trees 102, 103
Deer, Fallow 8, 16
    Red 16
    Roe 16
    Sika 16
Demoiselle 90
Deodar 107
Devil's coach horse 83
Dipper 49
Diver, Black-throated 22
Diving beetle, Great 83
Dock, Broad-leaved 155
Dolphin 7, 19
Dormouse 11
    Edible 11
Dotterel 21, 33
Dove, Collared 40
    Rock 40
    Stock 40
    Turtle 40
Dragonfly, Emperor 90
    Four-spotted 90
    Golden-ringed 90
Drinker moth 80
Dryad's saddle 182
Duck 24-26
    Tufted 25
    Eider 26
Dunlin 35
Dunnock 54

Eagle, Golden 28
Earth-ball 183
Earth star 183
Earthworm 92
Earwig 91
Eel 65, 67
Elder 135
Elder, Ground 154
Elk 17
Elm, English 104, 129
    Wych 129
Emerald Moth,
    Large 81

Emperor moth 80
Emperor, Purple 75
Evergreens 105-117
Eyebright 161

Fat hen 145
Fieldfare 50
Figwort 161
Finches 56-57
Fir, Douglas 108
    European silver 106
    Grand 107
Fishes 64-71
Flea, Cat 91
Flounder 70
Fly, Bee 88
    Crane 88
    House 88
    Hover 88
    Robber 88
    Stable 88
Fly agaric 175
Flycatcher,
    Pied 54
    Spotted 54
Forget-me-not, Field 158
Foxglove 160
Fox, Red 8, 13
Freshwater fishes 65-69
Fritillary, Heath 76
    Pearl-bordered 76
    Silver-washed 76
Frog, Common 62
    Edible 62
    European tree 60
Fulmar 22
Fumitory 141
Fungi 174-183
Fur beetle 83
Furniture beetle 84

Game birds 30-31
Gannet 22
Gentian, Field 157
Goat moth 82
Goat's-beard 168
Goat, Wild 17
Goby 71
Godwit, Bar-tailed 34
    Black-tailed 34
Goldcrest 53
Goldeneye 25
Goldfinch 56
Goosander 26
Goose, Brent 27
    Canada 27
    Pink-footed 27
Gorse 147
Goshawk 28
Grasshopper, Meadow 91
Grass of Parnassus 152
Grayling 66
Grebe, Great Crested 22
    Little 22
Greenfinch 56
Greenfly, Rose aphid 85
Greenshank 35

Greylag 27
Grisette, Tawny 175
Ground beetle,
    Violet 83
Groundsel 168
Grouse, Black 30
    Red 30
    Willow 30
Gudgeon 69
Guillemot 39
Gull, Black-headed 37
    Common 37
    Great black-backed 37
    Herring 37
    Lesser black-backed 37
    Little 37
    Mediterranean 37

Hairstreak, Green 78
    Purple 78
Harebell 163
Hare, Blue 9
    Brown 9
Harrier, Hen 28
    Marsh 28
Harvestman 92
Hawfinch 56
Hawkmoth,
    Death's head 79
    Hummingbird 79
    Lime 79
Hawthorn 131
Hazel 120
Hazelnut 31
Heath butterfly, Small 77
Heather 156
Hedgehog 12
Helleborine,
    Broad-leaved 173
Hemlock, Western 108
Herb robert 146
Heron 23
Hobby 29
Hogweed 154
Holly 135
Honey fungus 176
Honeysuckle 164
Hoopoe 42
Hopper, Frog 85
    Leaf 85
    Sand 100
Hornbeam 102, 103, 122
Hornet 87
Horn of plenty 176
Horntail 87

Ichneumon fly 87
Ink cap, Shaggy 181
Insects 72-73
Invertebrates 72-93
Iris, Yellow 172
Ivy 153
    Ground 162

Jackdaw 46
Jay 47
Jellyfish 95, 101

Jew's ear 183
Juniper 115

Kestrel 29
Kingfisher 21, 42
Kittiwake 38
Knot 35

Laburnum 134
Lacewing 89
Lackey moth 80
Ladybird, Seven-spot 84
Lady's smock 141
Lamprey, River 65
Lappet moth 80
Lapwing 33
Larch,
    European 105
    Japanese 105
Lark 45
    Crested 45
Leech, Medicinal 93
Lily-of-the-Valley 171
Lime, Common 128
    Small-leaved 128
Limpet, Common 96
    Keyhole 96
    Slipper 96
Linnet 56
Lizard, Common 61
    Green 60
    Sand 61
Loach, Stone 67
Lobster 95, 100
Loosestrife, Purple 152
Lords and ladies 171
Louse, Bark 91
Lugworm 101

Magpie 47
Magpie moth 81
Mallow, Common 145
Mammals 6-19
Maple, Field 126
    Norway 126
Marigold, Marsh 139
Marten, Beech 15
    Pine 15
Martin, House 45
    Sand 45
Mayfly 89
Mayweed, Scentless 166
Meadowsweet 150
Mealworm beetle 84
Mercury, Dogs 155
Merganser, Red-breasted 26
Merlin 29
Midge 88
Milk cap, Saffron 177
    Ugly 177
Milkwort, Common 142
Millipede 92
Minnow 69
Mint, Corn 162
Mite, Harvest 92
Mole 12
Molluscs 94, 95

Monkey puzzle see
    Chile pine
Moorhen 32
Mosquito 88
Moths 73, 79-82
Mouse, Harvest 11
    House 11
    Wood 11
Mullein, Great 161
Mushroom, Field 180
Muskrat 9
Mussel 98
Mycena, Milking 179

Necklace shell 96
Needle shell 97
Newt, Palmate 63
    Smooth 63
    Warty 63
Nightingale 51
Nightjar 42
Nightshade, Deadly 159
    Enchanter's 153
Nipplewort 169
Nuthatch 49
Nut shell 98
Nymph 72

Oak, Common 103, 124
    Cork 125
    Holm 123
    Sessile 124
    Turkey 125
Octopus 94
Oil beetle 84
Olive 135
Orange tip butterfly 74
Orchid, Early purple 173
Oriole, Golden 47
Ormer 97
Osprey 29
Otter 8, 13
Otter shell 98
Owl, Barn 21, 41
    Eagle 41
    Little 41
    Long-eared 41
    Pygmy 41
    Short-eared 41
    Tawny 41
Oyster fungus 179
Oystercatcher 33
Oyster 98
    Saddle 98

Painted lady butterfly 75
Palm, Chusan 117
    European Fan 117
Pansy, Wild 142
Parasol mushroom 175
    Shaggy 175
Partridge 31
Peacock butterfly 75
Pea family ◄134, 147, 148
Pelican's foot 96
Peppered moth 81
Perch 67

Peregrine 29
Periwinkle, Common 97
    Flat 97
Pheasant 31
Pholiota, Shaggy 180
Piddock 99
Pike 66
Pimpernel, Scarlet 157
Pine, Arolla 110
    Austrian 111
    Corsican 111
    Monterey 110
    Scots 111
    Swiss stone 110
    Weymouth 104, 111
Pintail 24
Pipistrelle 18
Pipit, Meadow 54
    Rock 54
    Tree 54
Plaice 70
Plane, London 104, 127
Plantain, Ribwort 163
Plover, Golden 33
    Little ringed 33
    Ringed 33
Plume moth 82
Pluteus, Common 180
Poached egg fungus 176
Pochard 25
Polecat 15
Policeman's helmet 146
Pondskater 85
Poplar, Black Italian 119
    Lombardy 118
    White 118
Poppy, Field 140
Porpoise 7, 19
Prawn 100
Praying mantis 73
Primrose 157
Ptarmigan 30
Puffin 39
Puss moth 79

Quail 31

Rabbit 8, 9
Radish, Wild 141
Ragged robin 143
Ragwort 95, 101
Ragwort 167
Rail, Water 32
Rat, Brown 11
Raven 46
Razorbill 39
Razor shell, Large 99
    Small 99
Redpoll 57
Redshank (bird) 35
Redshank (flower) 155
Redstart 21, 51
    Black 51
Redwing 50
Redwood 102
    Coast 113
    Dawn 112

Reptiles 60, 61
Restharrow 148
Ringlet butterfly 77
Roach 68
Robin 21, 51
Rodents 6, 10-11
Roller 42
Rook 46
Rose, Dog 149
Rose family 131-133, 149, 151
Rowan 131
Rudd 69
Ruff 36

St. George's mushroom 179
St. John's wort, Common 142
Salamander, Fire 63
Salmon 65, 66
Sand eel, Greater 71
Sanderling 35
Sand hopper 100
Sandpiper, Common 34
    Curlew 35
Sawfly, Hawthorn 87
Saxifrage, Rue-leaved 152
Scabious, Devil's bit 165
    Field 165
Scallop, Queen 98
Scorpion fish 71
Scorpion fly 89
Scoter 25
Seashore creatures 94-101
Seal 7,
    Common 19
    Grey 19
Sea slater 100
Sea urchin 95, 101
Self heal 162
Sequoia, Giant 112
Shag 23
Shank, Spindle 178
    Velvet 177
Shearwater, Manx 22
Shelduck 26
Shells 94-97
Shepherd's purse 141
Shield bug, Hawthorn 85
Shoveler 25
Shrew, Common 12
    Pygmy 12,
    Water 12
    White-toothed 12
Shrike, Great grey 55
    Red-backed 55
Shrimp 95, 100
Sickener, The 177
Silver birch 121
Silver fish 91
Silverweed 151
Silver Y moth 73
Siskin 56
Skipper, Grizzled 78
    Small 78
Skylark 45

Slow-worm 60, 61
Slug, Garden 93
    Great grey 93
Smelt, Sand 71
Smew 26
Snail, Garden 93
    Great pond 93
    Great ram's horn 93
Snake fly 89
Snake, Grass 61
    Smooth 61
Snipe 34
Snowdrop 172
Sorrel, Common 155
    Wood 145
Sow-thistle, Perennial 169
Sparrowhawk 28
Sparrow, House 59
    Italian House 59
    Rock 59
    Tree 59
Spear thistle 167
Spearwort, Lesser 138
Speedwell, Germander 160
Spider, Garden 92
    House 92
    Water 92
    Wolf 92
Spindle shank 178
Springtail 91
Spruce, Norway 102, 109
    Sitka 109
Spurrey, Corn 144
Squid 94
Squirrel,
    Grey 10, Red 10
Stag beetle 83
Starfish 95, 101
Starling 55
Stickleback,
    Ten spined 67
    Three spined 67
Stilt, Black-winged 36
Stitchwort, Greater 144
Stoat 14
Stonechat 51
Stonecrop, Biting 151
Stonefly 89
Stork, White 23
Strawberry, Wild 149
Sundew 152
Swallow 45
Swallowtail 74
Swamp cypress 113
Swan, Mute 27
    Whooper 27
Swift 42
Swift moth 82
Sycamore 103, 127

Tadpole 60
Teal 24
Tellin, Baltic 99
    Blunt 99
    Thin 99
Tench 68

Tern, Black 38
    Common 38
    Little 38
    Sandwich 38
Thistle, Spear 167
Thrift 156
Thrip, Onion 91
Thrush, Mistle 50
    Song 50
Tiger beetle,
    Green 83
Tiger moth, Garden 80
Tit, Bearded 49
    Blue 48
    Coal 48
    Great 48
    Long-tailed 48
    Marsh 48
    Willow 48
Toad, Common 62
    Midwife 62
    Natterjack 62
Toadflax, Common 161
Topshell, Painted 96
Tortoise beetle 84
Tortoiseshell butterfly,
    Small 76
Tortrix moth,
    Green 82
Tower shell 97
Tree creeper 49
Trees 102-135
Trefoil, Bird's foot 147
Trough shell, Rayed 99
Trout, Brown 66
    Rainbow 66
Turnstone 33
Tussock moth,
    Pale 80
Twayblade 173

Underwing, Red 81
    Yellow 81
Univalves 94

Valerian, Common 165
Venus shell, Striped 99
Verdigris fungus 181
Vetch, Tufted 148
Viper 60
Vole, Bank 10,
    Short-tailed 10,
    Water 10
Violet, Sweet 142

Waders 33-37
Wagtail, Grey 55
    Pied 55
Wall butterfly 77
Walnut 130
Warbler, Dartford 53
    Garden 52
    Reed 52
    Sedge 52
    Willow 53
    Wood 53

Wasp beetle 84
Wasp, Common 87
    Digger 87
    Gall 87
    Potter 87
Water boatman 85
Water crowfoot,
    Thread-leaved 139
Water-lily, White 140
    Yellow 140
Waxwing 55
Weasel 14
Wedge shell, Banded 99
Weevil, Nut 84
Wellingtonia *see*
    Sequoia, Giant
Wentletrap 97
Wheatear 50
Whelk 96
Whinchat 51
Whirligig beetle 83
Whitebeam 132
White butterfly, Large 74
    Marbled 77
    Small 74
Whitefly, Greenhouse 85
White moth,
    bordered 81
Whitethroat 53
Whiting 70
Wigeon 24
Wild cat 15
Wild flowers 136-173
Willow, Crack 119
    Goat 120
    White 119
Willowherb, Rosebay 153
Winkle, Sting 96
Wood butterfly, Speckled
    77
Woodcock 34
Woodlark 45
Woodlouse 93
Woodpecker, Black 43
    Great spotted 44
    Green 43
    Grey-headed 43
    Lesser spotted 44
    Middle spotted 44
    White-backed 44
Woodpigeon 40
Worms 95
Woundwort, Hedge 163
Wren 20, 49
Wryneck 43

Yarrow 170
Yellowhammer 58
Yew 104, 116

(Scientific Names)

Abies alba 106
    grandis 107
Abramis brama 68
Abraxas grossulariata 81
Acanthis cannabina 56
    flammea 57
*Acanthosoma
    haemorrhoidale 85*
Accipiter gentilis 28
    nisus 28
Acer campestre 126
    platanoides 126
    pseudoplatanus 127
Acherontia atropos 79
Acheta domesticus 91
Achillea millefolium 170
*Acrocephalus
    schoenobaenus 52*
    scirpaceus 52
Actinia equina 101
Aegithalos caudatus 48
*Aegopodium podagraria
    154*
*Aesculus hippocastanum
    128*
Agaricus campestris 181
Aglais urticae 76
Agrion virgo 90
Alauda arvensis 45
Alca torda 39
Alcedo atthis 42
Alces alces 17
Alnus glutinosa 5, 121
Alytes obstetricans 62
Amanita muscaria 175
    phalloides 175
Amanitopsis fulva 175
Ammodytes lanceolatus 71
Ammophila sabulosa 87
Anagallis arvensis 157
Anas acuta 24
    clypeata 25
    penelope 24
    platyrhynchos 24
Anax imperator 90
Andrena armata 86
Anemone nemorosa 139
Anguilla anguilla 67
Anguis fragilis 60, 61
Anobium punctatum 84
Anomia ephippium 98
Anser anser 27
    brachyrhynchus 27
Anthocharis cardamines 74
Anthriscus sylvestris 154
Anthus pratensis 54
    spinoletta 54
    trivialis 54
Apatura iris 75
Aphantopus hyperantus 77
Aphis fabae 85
Apis mellifera 86
Apodemus sylvaticus 11
Aporrhais pes-pelecani 96

Apus apus 42
Aquila chrysaetos 28
Araucaria araucana 116
Arctia caja 80
Arctium minus 167
Ardea cinerea 23
Arenaria interpres 33
Arenicola marina 101
Argynnis paphia 76
Argyroneta aquatica 92
Arion subfuscus 93
Armeria maritima 156
Armillaria mellea 176
Arum maculatum 171
Arvicola terrestris 10
Asilus crabroniformis 88
Asio flammeus 41
    otus 41
Asterias rubens 101
Aster tripolium 166
Ataneus diadematus 92
Athene noctua 41
Atherina presbyter 71
Atropa bella-donna 159
Attagenus pellio 83
Aurelia aurita 101
*Auricularia auricula-judae
    183*
Aythya ferina 25
Aythya fuligula 25

Balanus balanoides 100
Barbus barbus 69
Bellis perennis 166
Betula pendula 121
Biorrhiza pallida 87
Biston betularia 81
Bittium reticulatum 97
Blatta orientalis 91
Blennius montagui 71
Blicca bjoerkna 68
Bombus lucorum 86
Bombycilla garrulus 55
Botaurus stellaris 23
Branta bernicla 27
    canadensis 27
Bubo bubo 41
Buccinum undatum 96
Bucephala clangula 25
Bufo bufo 62
Bufo calamita 62
Bupalus piniaria 81
Burhinus oedicnemus 36
Buteo buteo 28

Calidris alba 35
    alpina 35
    canutus 35
    ferruginea 35
Callimorpha jacobaeae 80
Calliostoma zizyphinum 96
Calliphora vomitoria 88
Callophrys rubi 78
Calluna vulgaris 156
Caltha palustris 139
Calyptraea chinensis 96
Calystegia sepium 159

Campanula rotundifolia 163
Cantharellus cibarius 176
Capra hircus 17
Capreolus capreolus 16
Caprimulgus europaeus 42
Caprinus betulus 122
Capsella bursa-pastoris 141
Carabus violaceus 83
Carcinus maenas 101
Cardamine pratensis 141
Cardium edule 98
Carduelis carduelis 56
    chloris 56
    spinus 56
Cassida viridis 84
Castanea sativa 123
Catocala nupta 81
Cedrus atlantica 106
    libani 107
Cerastium holosteoides 143
Certhia familiaris 49
Cerura vinula 79
Cervus elaphus 16
    nippon 16
Chamaecyparis
    lawsoniana 114
Chamaerops humilis 117
Charadrius dubius 33
    hiaticula 33
Chelidonium majus 140
Chenopodium album 145
Chironomus annularis 88
Chlamys opercularis 98
Chlidonias niger 38
Chorthippus parallelus 91
Chrysopa septempunctata
    89
Cicadetta montana 85
Cicindela campestris 83
Ciconia ciconia 23
Cinclus cinclus 49
Circaea lutetiana 153
Circus aeruginosus 28
    cyaneus 28
Cirsium vulgare 167
Clathrus clathrus 97
Clavulina cristata 183
Clethrionomys glareolus 10
Clitocybe nebularis 177
Clossiana euphrosyne 76
Clytus arietis 84
Coccinella 7-punctata 84
Coccothraustes
    coccothraustes 56
Coenonympha pamphilus
    77
Colias crocea 74
Collybia fusipes 178
Columba livia 40
    oenas 40
    palumbus 40
Convallaria majalis 171
Coprinus comatus 181
Coracias garrulus 42
Cordulegaster boltonii 90
Coriolus versicolor 182
Corixa punctata 85

Coronella austriaca 61
Cortinarius pseudosalor 180
Corvus corax 46
    corone cornix 46
    corone corone 46
    frugilegus 46
    monedula 46
Corylus avellana 120
Corymbites cupreus 83
Cossus cossus 82
Cottus gobio 67
Coturnix coturnix 31
Crangon vulgaris 99
Crataegus monogyna 131
Craterellus cornucopioides
    176
Crepidula fornicata 96
Crex crex 32
Crocidura russula 12
Cryptomeria japonica 113
Ctenocephalides felis 91
Cuculus canorus 40
Culex pipiens 88
Cupido minimus 78
Cupressocyparis leylandii
    114
Cupressus macrocarpa 114
    sempervirens 115
Curculio nucum 84
Cydia pomonella 82
Cygnus cygnus 27
    olor 27
Cyprinus carpio 68

Dama dama 16
Dasychira pudibunda 80
Delichon urbica 45
Delphinus delphis 7, 19
Dendrocopos leucotos 44
    major 44
    medius 44
    minor 44
Dicentrarchus labrax 70
Digitalis purpurea 160
Donax vittatus 99
Dosinia exoleta 98
Drosera rotundifolia 152
Dryocopus martius 43
Dysticus marginalis 83

Echinus esculentus 101
Echium vulgare 158
Emberiza calandra 58
    cia 59
    citrinella 58
    cirlus 58
    hortulana 58
    schoeniclus 59
Ensis ensis 99
    siliqua 99
Epilobium angustifolium
    153
Epipactis helleborine 173
Erinaceus europaeus 12
Erithacus rubecula 21, 51
Esox lucius 66
Eudromias morinellus 33

Eumenes pendunculatus 87
Eupagurus bernhardus 101
Eupatorium cannabinum
    170
Euphrasia officinalis 161

Fagus sylvatica 122
Falco columbarius 29
    peregrinus 29
    subbuteo 29
    tinnunculus 29
Felis silvestris 15
Ficedula hypoleuca 54
Filipendula ulmaria 150
Fissurella costaria 96
Fistulina hepatica 174
Flammulina velutipes 177
Forficula auricularia 91
Formica fusca 86
    rufa 86
Fragaria vesca 149
Fratercula arctica 39
Fraxinus excelsior 130
    ornus 130
Fringilla coelebs 57
Fulica atra 32
Fumaria officinalis 141

Gadus morhua 70
Galerida cristata 45
Galanthus nivalis 172
Galium aparine 164
    verum 164
Gallinago gallinago 34
Gallinula chloropus 32
Garrulus glandarius 47
Gasterosteus aculeatus 67
Gastropacha quercifolia 80
Gavia arctica 22
Geastrum triplex 183
Gentianella campestris 157
Geometra papilionaria 81
Geranium pratense 146
    robertianum 146
Gerris lacustris 85
Geum rivale 151
Glaucidium passerinum 41
Glechoma hederacea 162
Glis glis 11
Glycymeris glycymeris 98
Gobio gobio 69
Gonepteryx rhamni 74
Grus grus 32
Gryllus campestris 91
Gymnopilus junonius 180
Gyrinus natator 83

Halichoerus grypus 19
Haliotis tuberculata 97
Haematopus ostralegus 33
Hedera helix 153
Helix aspersa 93
Hepialus lupulina 82
Heracleum sphondylium
    154
Himantopus himantopus 36
Hirudo medicinalis 93

Hirundo rustica 45
Homarus vulgaris 100
Hyacinthoides non-scripta
    171
Hydnum repandum 183
Hygrophorus coccineus 179
Hyla meridionalis 60
Hypericum perforatum 142
Hypholoma fasciculare 181

Ilex aquifolium 135
Impatiens glandulifera 146
Inachis io 75
Inocybe geophylla 181
Iris pseudacorus 172
Isonychia ignota 89

Jassus lanio 85
Juglans regia 130
Jynx torquilla 43

Knautia arvensis 165

Laccaria amethystea 178
    laccata 178
Lacerta agilis 61
    vivipara 61
    viridis 60
Lactarius deliciosus 177
    turpis 177
Lagopus lagopus 30
    mutus 30
    scoticus 30
Lamium album 162
Lampetra fluviatilis 65
Lanius collurio 55
    excubitor 55
Lapsana communis 169
Larix decidua 105
    kaempferi 105
Larus argentatus 37
    canus 37
    fuscus 37
    marinus 37
    ridibundus 37
Lasiommata megera 77
Lasius niger 86
Leander serratus 100
Lepidochitona cinereus
    97
Lepiota procera 175
    rhacodes 175
Lepisma saccharina 91
Lepista nuda 178
Lepus capensis 9
    timidus 9
Leuciscus leuciscus 68
Libellula quadrimaculata
    90
Ligia oceanica 100
Limanda limanda 70
Limax maximus 93
Limenitis camilla 75
Limosa lapponica 34
    limosa 34
Linaria vulgaris 161
Listera ovata 173

Lithobius forficatus 92
Littorina littoralis 97
    littorea 97
Lonicera periclymenum
    164
Lotus corniculatus 147
Loxia curvirostra 57
Lucanus cervus 83
Lullula arborea 45
Lumbricus terrestris 92
Luscinia megarhynchos 51
    svecica 51
Lutra lutra 13
Lutraria lutraria 98
Lycaena phlaeas 78
Lymnaea stagnalis 93
Lyrurus tetrix 30
Lythrum salicaria 152

Macroglossum
    stellatarum 79
Macrosiphum rusae 85
Mactra corallina 99
Malacosoma neustria 80
Malus sylvestris 132
Malva sylvestris 145
Maniola jurtina 77
Mantis religiosa 73
Marasmius oreades 178
Martes martes 15
Matricaria maritima 166
Megachile centuncularis 86
Melampyrum pratense 160
Melanargia galathea 77
Melanitta nigra 25
Meles meles 6, 8, 13
Mellicta athalia 76
Meloe proscarabaeus 84
Melolontha melolontha 83
Mentha arvensis 162
Menyanthes trifoliata 159
Mercurialis perennis 155
Mergus albellus 26
    merganser 26
    serrator 26
Merops apiaster 42
Metasequoia
    glyptostroboides 112
Micromys minutus 11
Microtus agrestis 10
Mimas tiliae 79
Motacilla alba 55
    cinerea 55
Musca domestica 88
Muscardinus
    avellanarius 11
Muscicapa striata 54
Mus musculus 11
Mustela erminea 14
    nivalis 14
    putorius 15
Mycena galopus 179
Myocastor coypus 9
Myosotis arvensis 158
Myotis daubentoni 18
    mystacinus 18
    nattereri 18

Mytilus edulis 98

Narcissus pseudo-
    narcissus 172
Natica alderi 96
Natrix natrix 61
Necrophorus humator 83
Neomys fodiens 12
Nereis diversicolor 101
Noctua pronuba 81
Noemacheilus
    barbatulus 67
Nomada lineola 86
Nucula nucleus 98
Numenius arquata 34
Nuphar lutea 140
Nyctalus noctula 18
Nymphaea alba 140
Nymphalis antiopa 76

Ocenebra erinacea 96
Ocypus olens 83
Oenanthe oenanthe 50
Olea europaea 135
Ommatoiulus sabulosus
    92
Ondatra zibethicus 9
Oniscus asellus 93
Ononis repens 148
Orchestia gammarella 100
Orchis mascula 173
Oriolus oriolus 47
Oryctolagus cuniculus 9
Ostrea edulis 98
Oudemansiella mucida
    176
Oxalis acetosella 145

Palinurus vulgaris 95
Pandion haliaetus 29
Panorpa communis 89
Panurus biarmicus 49
Papaver rhoeas 140
Papilio machaon 74
Pararge aegeria 77
Parnassia palustris 152
Parus ater 48
    caeruleus 48
    major 48
    montanus 48
    palustris 48
Passer domesticus 59
    montanus 59
Patella vulgata 96
Perca fluviatilis 67
Perdix perdix 31
Perlodes microcephala 89
Petasites hybridus 170
Petronia petronia 59
Phalacrocorax aristotelis 23
    carbo 23
Phalangium opilio 92
Phalera bucephala 79
Phasianus colchicus 31
Philaenus spumarius 85
Philomachus pugnax 36
Philudoria potatoria 80
Phocaena phocaena 7, 19

190

Phoca vitulina 7, 19
Phoenicurus ochruros 51
  phoenicurus 51
Pholas dactylus 99
Pholiota aurivella 180
  squarrosa 180
Phoxinus phoxinus 69
Phryganea grandis 89
Phylloscopus collybita 53
  sibilatrix 53
  trochilus 53
Pica pica 47
Picea abies 109
  sitchensis 109
Picus canus 43
  viridis 43
Pieris brassicae 74
  rapae 74
Pinus cembra 110
  nigra var. nigra 111
    var. maritima 111
  radiata 110
  strobus 111
  sylvestris 111
Pipistrellus pipistrellus 18
Piptoporus betulinus 182
Pisaura listera 92
Planorbarius corneus 93
Plantago lanceolata 163
Platanus x hispanica 127
Platichthys flesus 70
Plecotus auritus 18
Plectrophenax nivalis 58
Pleuronectes platessa 70
Pleurotus ostreatus 179
Pluteus cervinus 180
Plusia gamma 73
Pluvialis apricaria 33
Podiceps cristatus 22
Podura aquatica 91
Polygala vulgaris 142
Polygonia c-album 76
Polygonum persicaria 155
Polyommatus icarus 78
Polyporus squamosus 182
Pomatoschistus microps 71
Populus euramericana
    var. serotina 119
  nigra var. italica 118
  tremula 118
Porzana porzana 32
Potentilla anserina 151
Primula vulgaris 157
Prunella modularis 54
  vulgaris 162
Prunus avium 133
  dulcis 133
  padus 133
Pseudotsuga
  menziesii 108
Pterophorus
  pentadactylus 82
Puffinus puffinus 22
Pyrgus malvae 78
Pyrochroa coccinea 84
Pyrrhocorax pyrrhocorax
    47

Pyrrhosoma nymphula 90
Pyrrhula pyrrhula 20, 57

Quercus cerris 125
  ilex 123
  petraea 124
  robur 124
  suber 125
Quercusia quercus 78

Rallus aquaticus 32
Rana esculenta 62
  temporaria 62
Ranunculus acris 138
  ficaria 138
  flammula 138
  trichophyllus 139
Raphanus raphanistrum
    141
Raphidia notata 89
Rattus norvegicus 11
Recurvirostra avosetta 36
Reduvius personatus 85
Regulus regulus 53
Rhinolophus
  ferrum-equinum 18
Rhyssa persuasoria 87
Riparia riparia 45
Rissa tridactyla 38
Robinia pseudoacacia 134
Rosa canina 149
Rubus fruticosus 150
Rumex acetosa 155
  obtusifolius 155
Russula emetica 177
Rutilus rutilus 68

Salamander salamandra 63
Salix alba 119
  capraea 120
  fragilis 119
Salmo gairdneri 66
  salar 66
  trutta 66
Sambucus nigra 135
Sarothamnus scopasius
    147
Saturnia pavonia 80
Saxicola rubetra 51
  torquata 51
Saxifraga tridactylites 152
Scardinius
  erythrophthalmus 69
Sciurus carolinensis 10
  vulgaris 10
Scleroderma citrinum 183
Scolopax rusticola 34
Scrophularia nodosa 161
Sedum acre 151
Senecio jacobaea 167
  vulgaris 168
Sepia officinalis 101
Sequoiadendron
  giganteum 112
Sequoia sempervirens 113

Sesia apiformis 82
Sialis lutaria 89
Silene dioica 143
Sitta europaea 49
Solanum dulcamara 159
Somateria mollissima 26
Sonchus arvensis 169
Sorbus aria 132
  aucuparia 131
Sorex araneus 12
  minutus 12
Spergula arvensis 144
Spilosoma lutea 80
Squalius leuciscus 69
Stachys sylvatica 163
Stellaria holostea 144
  media 144
Sterna albifrons 38
  hirundo 38
  sandvicensis 38
Streptopelia decaocto 40
  turtur 40
Strix aluco 41
Stropharia aeruginosa 181
Sturnus vulgaris 55
Succisa pratense 165
Suillus grevillei 182
Sula bassana 22
Sus scrofa 17
Sylvia atricapilla 52
  borin 52
  communis 53
  undata 53
Symphytum officinale 158
Syrphus ribesi 88

Tachybaptus ruficollis 22
Tadorna tadorna 26
Talpa europaea 12
Taraxacum officinale 168
Taurulus bubalis 71
Taxodium distichum 113
Taxus baccata 116
Tealia felina 101
Tegenaria domestica 92
Tenebrio molitor 84
Tetrao urogallus 30
Tetrastes bonasia 31
Tettigonia viridissima 91
Thrips tabaci 91
Thuja plicata 115
Thymallus thymallus 66
Thymelicus sylvestris 78
Tilia cordata 128
  europaea 128
Tinca tinca 68
Tipula maxima 88
Tortrix viridana 82
Trachycarpus fortunei 117
Tragopogon pratensis 168
Trialeurodes
  vaporariorum 85
Trichiosoma tibiale 87
Tricholoma gambosum
    178
Trifolium pratense 148
  repens 148

Tringa hypoleucos 34
    nebularia 35
    totanus 35
Triturus cristatus 63
    helveticus 63
    vulgaris 63
Trivia monacha 97
Troglodytes
    troglodytes 49
Trombicula
    autumnalis 92
Tsuga heterophylla 108
Turdus iliacus 50
    merula 50
    philomelos 50
    pilaris 50
    viscivorus 50

Turritella communis 97
Tussilago farfara 169
Tyto alba 21, 41

Ulex europaeus 147
Ulmus glabra 129
    procera 129
Upupa epops 42
Uria aalge 39
Urocerus gigas 87
Urtica dioica 156

Vaccinium myrtillus 156
Valeriana officinalis 165
Vanellus vanellus 33
Vanessa atalanta 75
    cardui 75

Venus striatula 99
Verbascum thapsus 161
Veronica chamaedrys 160
Vespa crabro 87
Vespula vulgaris 87
Vicia cracca 148
Viola odorata 142
    tricolor 142
Vipera berus 61
Vulpes vulpes 13

Xanthorhoe fluctuata 81
Xestobium rufovillosum 84

Zygaena filipendulae 82

ACKNOWLEDGEMENTS

The publishers wish to thank the following people for their help in supplying artwork and photographs for this book:

Artwork: Norma Birgin, Wendy Bramall, Terry Callcut, Martin Camm, Bernard Robinson, Rod Sutterby, David Wright.

Photographs: Heather Angel 65, 73; Joe Blossom/NHPA 6; Michael Chinery 60; Stephen Dalton/NHPA 4; Sonia Halliday 104 top right; Brian Hawkes/NHPA 60, 89, Ken Merrylees 104 top centre, bottom left and right; Maurice Nimmo 5, 104 bottom centre.

Picture Research: Penny Warn.